GLOSSARY

NEMONIK THINKING

Second Edition

Dr. Auke Schade

nemonik-thinking.org

Copyright

Second Edition
Published 1 July 2016
@ nemonik-thinking.org
ISBN 978-0-473-35501-2

Abstract

Nemonik thinking is a competitive advantage because it mobilizes your hidden genius, accelerates your thinking, improves your memory, prevents blind-spots, and reveals opportunities, while its constant preparedness reduces stress levels. Definitions associated with the mind and reality are inherently hypothetical, fuzzy, and intertwined. Nevertheless, to improve our understanding of the way we think, we have to identify, differentiate, and define those components. Therefore, this glossary provides descriptions for the concepts associated with nemonik thinking. To become skilled in nemonik thinking, it is recommended to study—*Think Smarter with Nemonik Thinking (Schade, 2016)*.

Dr. Auke Schade

My life started during the devastation of World War II. As a teenager, I worked as a carpenter and studied building engineering at night school. During the seventies, I became a financial manager for a multinational corporation, ran my own business, and studied economics in my spare time. My interest in the psychology of management extended to the interaction between the mind, body, and reality. In 1980, I immigrated to New Zealand where I obtained a doctorate in psychology from the University of Auckland. My mission is to make people the smartest thinkers they can be, which has led me to the development of nemonik thinking.[i]

Reality shows that humanity's way of thinking is failing dramatically. As a result, the next generation is facing overpopulation, dwindling resources, nuclear warfare, industrial pollution, climate change, etc. Therefore, they have to become the best thinkers they can be.

Download free eBooks and videos
@ nemonik-thinking.org

---

i Appendix: Nemonik Thinking.

Notes

_____

_____

_____

_____

_____

_____

_____

_____

_____

_____

_____

_____

_____

CONTENTS

DIAGRAM NEMONIK THINKING

Nemonik thinking
    Mind
        Conscious
            Rational thinking
                OBJECTIVE-1
                COLLECTIVE-2
        Subconscious
            Affectorial thinking
                CREATIVE-3
                REACTIVE-4
    Reality
            Space
                ADVANCE-5
                STAY-6
                RETREAT-7
            Matter
                ACCUMULATE-8
                PRESERVE-9
                DISPOSE-10
            Time
                ACT-11
                WAIT-12
                PREPARE-13
    Interaction
            Perception
                ACCEPT-14
                REJECT-15
            Projection
                REVEAL-16
                CONCEAL-17

Notes

GLOSSARY

#

80/20 rule—in 20% of the time required doing a perfect job; people are able to complete 80% of that job to a reasonable standard. The remaining 80% of their time will be spent on perfecting the last 20% of that job. If the rule applies, then you could complete 80% of five jobs to a reasonable standard (400%) in the same time required to complete one job perfectly (100%). Hence, if the quality of the jobs is limited to 80%, then the total quantity would increase from 100 to 400%. Therefore, it is productive to evaluate the need for quantity and quality—set clear goals and priorities—and use time management in order to achieve them. See Prepare.

A

Abnormal—collective judgement that a person's internal reality is outside the collectively accepted perception of the sensory reality. Antonym—Normal. See Collective.

Accelerator—See Nemonik-accelerator.

Accept—perceptual nemonik that prompts the mind to accept the incoming information as a true description of the sensory reality. One can adopt a strict or lax decision criterion. Keywords for accept include: accord, agree, approve, believe, careless, comply, confident, converted, convinced, correct, credulous, faith, gullible, incoming information, influenced, lax criterion, naive, perception, persuaded, susceptible, swayed, true, trust, etc. Antonym—Reject. See Perception.

Accumulate—material nemonik that prompts the mind to increase the amount of matter that is under control. Keywords for accumulate include: accrue, acquire, add, amalgamate, amass, annex, assemble, borrow, buy, collect, construct, cultivate, develop, earn, enlarge, forage, gain, greed, grow, hire, hoard, invest, manufacture, matter, obtain, procure, produce, purchase, raid, seize, steal, take, etc. See Matter.

Act—temporal nemonik that prompts the mind to change or move matter in space and time. Keywords for act include: accept, accumulate, advance, carry out, conceal, create, dispose, do, execute, go, move, perform, prepare, preserve, react, recall, reject, respond, retreat, reveal, rule, stay, wait, etc. See Time.

Active listening—listening with the intent to understand, rather than to respond. Active listeners use questions, paraphrasing, and positive body language. It is a mistake to assume that an active listener will agree, obey, or subordinate, just because that person is listening. Collecting information cost time and effort. Therefore, the subconscious has a tendency to defend the accepted information and use talking and passive silence in order to block new information. See Groupthink and Cognitive dissonance.

Adam Smith—See Smith, Adam.

Advance—spatial nemonik that prompts the mind to decrease the distance to the goal. Keywords for advance include: assault, attack, challenge, charge, chase, conquer, develop, enter, expansion, explore, forward, infiltrate, invade, move ahead, offensive, penetrate, progress, promote, pursue, push, seize, space, storm, strike, etc. See Space.

Affecters—mental signals that are generated by subconscious affectorial thinking, which influence the conscious without explaining the underlying subconscious processes. Affecters do not rely on conscious reasoning or facts, and therefore, they are by definition non-rational and illogical. However, affecters are sometimes rationalised. Affecters can be divided into creative affecters and reactive affecters. Affecters include beliefs, desires, discoveries, emotions, fantasies, habits, heuristics, ideas, impulses, innovations, insights, inspirations, intuitions, inventions, novelties, reactions, reflexes, routines, skills, etc. See Affectorial thinking.

Affectorial bias—consistent preference for affectorial thinking that is independent of the situation in the sensory reality.

Affectorial thinking—subconscious part of nemonik thinking that deals with the unpredictable chaos of reality by generating affecters that influence the conscious. Affecters are mental signals that are generated by subconscious affectorial thinking, which influence the conscious without explaining the underlying subconscious processes. Affecters include beliefs, desires, discoveries, emotions, fantasies, habits, heuristics, ideas, impulses, innovations, insights, inspirations, intuitions, inventions, novelties, reactions, reflexes, routines, skills, etc. The mental processes underlying affectorial thinking are outside the conscious awareness. Hence, they cannot be observed directly and, therefore, affectorial thinking appears non-rational and irrational to the rational conscious. This is not to say that affectorial thinking is without reason. We just do not know the underlying processes, because they are hidden in the subconscious. The word 'irrational' has often been used as a negative label to discredit affectorial thinking. Furthermore, meditation, relaxation, and a silent mind foster subconscious dominance and affectorial thinking. The opposite of affectorial thinking is rational thinking. Herbert Spencer introduced the unknown and known. These, concepts underlie the division of affectorial thinking into respectively the creative (unknown) and reactive mindmodes (known). Dyslexia and koans might foster affectorial thinking. However, more research is required. Keywords for affectorial thinking include: affecters, chaos, contradictory, disorder, drowsy, illogical, inconsistent, meditation, noncritical, non-rational, prejudiced, reflection, relaxation, silent mind, sleep, subconscious, subjective, trust, turmoil, unfounded, unpredictable, unreasonable, unscientific, unsystematic, etc. In the context of Lao Zi's philosophy, affectorial thinking could be called *Yin* thinking. Antonym—Rational thinking. See Subconscious.

Algorithm—set of rules comprising a computational procedure, which follows a definite path to the single solution of a problem. See Mindsets.

Aligning with harmonisations (Chinese *shun qi*)—moving in the same direction as *Qi* when this inexhaustible force is harmonising the *Yin-Yang* balance. Aligning is the second of the three fundamental alignments with the Way (*Dao*). During the harmonisation of the *Yin-Yang* balance, the un-limited force of the Way provides free energy that we can use to our advantage. Instead of rowing upstream, sages drift with the flow of the water to their destination. The natural virtue of humility is one of Lao Zi's three treasures and part of aligning with harmonisation. See LaoZi and *Dao De Jing*.

Aligning with *Qi*—See Aligning with harmonisations.

Aligning with the Way (Chinese *shun dao*)—aiming for the right goals, while being in the right place, at the right time, with the right resources and in the right state of mind. This requires Non-action; Affectorial thinking; Maintain-ing the *Yin-Yang* balance; Aligning with Harmonisations; and Restoring the *Yin-Yang* balance. See LaoZi and *Dao De Jing*.

Alignment—positioning in order to take optimal advantage of the Way (*Dao*). Alignment is the constant of the sages. See Aligning with the Way and Three fundamental align-ments.

All-inclusive—See Exhaustive.

All-things (Chinese *wan wu*)—literally ten thousand things or just a great number of things. All-things refer to the myri-ad of organic and inorganic things that exist in the sensory reality. See LaoZi and *Dao De Jing*.

Analects—book comprising the ideas of Confucius, which were compiled by his students after his death. See Confu-cius.

Anaximander (610-545 BC)—Greek philosopher who suggested that apeiron was the physical origin of all substances. See Greek philosophers.

Anaximenes (fl. c. 545 BC)—Greek philosopher who suggested that air was the origin of all substances. See Greek philosophers.

Ancients (Chinese *gu*)—sages of antiquity that Lao Zi refers to in *Dao De Jing*. See LaoZi, and *Dao De Jing*.

Answering—See SCARRED.

Antimatter—particles that are mirror images of the particles comprising the ordinary matter as known in the sensory reality. Anti-particles have the same mass as ordinary particles but opposite electromagnetic properties. Antimatter might be similar to Lao Zi's idea of Non-existence. Antonym—Matter. See LaoZi and *Dao De Jing*.

Antithesis—tested description of reality that contradicts a thesis. Antonym—Thesis. See Hegel.

Anti-Universe—hypothetical alternative or parallel Universe that contains exclusively antimatter and is a mirror image of our Universe. Lao Zi's division of Nothing in Existence and Non-existence supports the hypothesis of an Anti-Universe. See Lao Zi and *Dao De Jing*.

Apeiron—indefinite substance hypothesised by Anaximander that cannot be perceived directly. It is an unlimited mass that does not change, but yields material from which all other substances are derived and as such, it is the primordial element of all substances. This idea has similarities with Max Planck's quanta and the recent God particle.

Aphorisms—folk wisdoms, heuristics, rules of thumb, truisms, clichés, definitions, mottos, and proverbs. See Informal logic.

Archetype of *Yang*—mass-energy. See *Yin, Yang,* Lao Zi, and *Dao De Jing.*

Archetype of *Yin*—gravitational-energy. See *Yan, Yin,* Lao Zi, and *Dao De Jing.*

Aristotle (384-322 BC)—Greek philosopher who developed the validity rules for reason, which form the basis for rational thinking. Those rules are part of formal logic and they lead our thinking from true facts to true conclusions about reality. In turn, those conclusions become the new facts and so on. His ideas broke the hold of mythology on the mind as the major source of explanations, changing irreversibly our mental and physical world. Aristotle's writings about logic were compiled by the Peripatetics—under the name Organon, or Instrument. Aristotle assumed that there is order in the universe and, therefore, that it is predictable. Modern civilization would not exist without the ideas of Aristotle. His logic arguments are the basis for all the sciences and the writing of computer software. See Greek philosophers, Rational thinking, and Reason.

Arrogant people—are in an orbit around their own ego and regard themselves as superior. They overestimate their own abilities and underestimate the size of their problems. Their ego resists and challenges every potential opposition. They are predictable and inflexible. Arrogant people perish, because they are unable to align with the unstoppable Way (Chinese *Dao*). Antonym—Humble. See LaoZi and *Dao De Jing.*

Art of Living—See Scientific Art of Living.

Art of War—See The Art of War.

Artefacts—manmade objects such as paintings, pianos, satellites, computers and the book you are reading right now. Whether ugly or beautiful, each artefact forms a recognisable pattern that is the result of human craft. See Artificial.

Artificial—refers to that part of the sensory reality that is manmade. Although we are an inevitable part of nature, intellect seems to set us apart from the rest of nature. In order to indicate that elusive distinction, we may refer to manmade objects and our interference with nature as being artificial. Antonym—Natural. See Collective mindmode.

Artificial facts—changeable facts that are only true within a particular collective because they are based on collective decisions. Antonym—Natural facts. See Collective mindmode.

Artificial knowledge—knowledge about the artificial rules of a collective. These rules are manmade and, therefore artificial knowledge is subjective, changeable, and temporary. Nemonik thinking incorporates artificial knowledge (collective). Artificial knowledge is used by solicitors, judges, police officers, accountants, politicians, militarists, and bureaucracy. Antonym—Natural knowledge. See Confucius and Collective mindmode.

Artificial rules—descriptions of the changeable cause-effect relationships that are only true within a particular collective, because they are based on decisions of that collective. Artificial rules are made by people for people. Artificial rules are subjective and moralistic, because what is the law in one collective might be a crime in another. Artificial rules include criminal, civil, and commercial rules, agreements, consents, contracts, creeds, customs, doctrines, dogmas, morals, rituals, social agreements, traditions, treaties, etc. Antonym—Natural rules. See Collective mindmode.

Artificial sensors—developed by scientists in order to explore the external reality beyond the sensory reality.

Artificial virtue—competence to align with the Confucian temporary Way of the People. Artificial virtue is based on the application of artificial rules. However, in Lao Zi's philosophy, artificial virtue is associated with people who are the lowest Greatness in the hierarchy of the Universe. In contrast, natural virtue is associated with people who align with the eternal Natural Way (*Dao*), which is the highest Greatness in the hierarchy of the Universe. Therefore, artificial virtue is inferior to natural virtue. Antonym—Natural virtue. See Collective mindmode.

Artificial way—temporary, changeable, and subjective way of artificial rules and knowledge that is created by people for people. Antonym—Natural way. See Collective mindmode.

Association—spontaneous mental jump from one concept to another related concept that is stored in the memory. For example, thinking about your kitchen might remind you of the dirty dishes in the sink—while they remind you of last night's party—with might lead you to think about your best friend—etc. This chain could be written as: kitchen / dishes / party / friend /etc. In computer terminology, that associative process is called hyper-linking. See Memory.

Atoms—primordial particles comprising all substances that were hypothesized by the Greek philosopher Democratis.

Atoms are compact, indivisible, infinite in number, but differ in shape and size. See Greek philosophers.

Audio spatial perception—conscious perception of space that is created subconsciously by integrating the different sounds that are perceived by each ear.

Auto-balance—dynamic balance between the state of the mind and the state of the body, which moves on a continuum ranging from tension to relaxation. See Nemonik meditation.

B

Balance—See Harmony.

Behaviour—the observable physical activity of an organism. See Psychology.

Being Named—See Naming.

Belief—acceptance of an untestable description of reality. Belief is associated with Spencer's concept of the unknowable. Antonym—Facts. See Reactive mindmode.

Beneficial harmonisations—See Productive harmonisations.

Benevolence (Chinese *ren*)—Confucian artificial virtue that maintains imbalances in collective. In terms of Confucian philosophy, benevolence is the love for one's fellow men. To be benevolent, it is essential that we do not impose on others what we do not desire for ourselves. Benevolence is associated with a social class called '*gentleman*'. This fosters division by creating a 'them and us' mentality. See Confucius, Artificial virtue, Collective thinking.

Big Bang—theory that there was a huge explosion some 10 to 20 billion years ago. There seems to be some consensus among physicists that the Big Bang heralded the formation of our Universe. In terms of Lao Zi's theory, this might have been a manifestation of the first division of Nothingness into Existence and Non-existence. Antonym—Big Crunch. See LaoZi and *Dao De Jing*.

Big Crunch—theory that in billions of years the Universe might contract as a result of the gravitational force that celestial bodies exert on each other. If there is enough matter in the Universe then it is closed. In that case, the gravitational pull in the Universe would be strong enough to decelerate the expansion of the Universe so that it may eventually contract. If there is insufficient matter in the Universe then there is not enough gravity to contract all that matter back into one point. In that case, the Universe is open and its expansion may go on forever. Antonym— Big Bang.

Bilateral thinking—nemonik thinking incorporates two complementary ways of thinking in order to cope with the order and chaos of the perceived dual reality. In accord, the conscious generates rational thinking to deal with the perceived order of reality, while the larger subconscious generates affectorial thinking to deal with the perceived chaos of reality.

Billion—one thousand million (1,000,000,000).

Binary thinking—false perception that thinking is a forced choice between two options.

Bing Fa (Chinese)—See The Art of War.

Bingfa (Chinese)—See The Art of War.

Biofeedback—learning process to control consciously an auditory or optical feedback signal that represents a subconsciously regulated physical process. See Nemonik meditation.

Black hole—gigantic star that has collapsed after it exhausted its nuclear energy. As a dimensionless object of infinite density, the gravity of a black hole is so large that even light cannot escape it. We can only see a sphere of darkness in space, called the event-horizon. Although no one knows precisely what a black hole contains, we might speculate that the enormous gravity of the black hole would crush all atoms and even fuse the sub-atomic particles. Such singularity might be Lao Zi's concept of Oneness. See LaoZi and Dao De Jing.

Blank mind—See Silent mind.

Blitzkrieg—coordinated high-speed military advance that fosters momentum, internal assistance, bypasses obstacles, and concentrates on the ultimate goal. This strategy was designed by Heinz Wilhelm Guderian. See Strategy.

Body—material part of a person, which is composed of organic cells and substances that are organised into a living system. See Mind, body, and spirit.

Bonaparte, Napoleon (1769-1821)—French emperor and military strategist. See Strategy.

Bono de—See de Bono.

Boxers—collective of Chinese nationalists called the 'Righteous and Harmonious Fist'. They rebelled against the foreigners who controlled China in the late 19th and early 20th century. They understood incorrectly from Lao Zi's *Dao De Jing* that sages are invulnerable. Therefore, they were reckless in combat. However, Lao Zi wrote that sages should avoid danger. See LaoZi and *Dao De Jing*.

Brainstorming—non-critical group technique that creates random ideas by fostering a silent mind, free expression, disorganization, and association, while inhibiting rational thinking. See Creative mindmode.

Brainware—set of self-organizing organic components and processes that support the mindware. In computer terminology, brainware could be compared to the hardware of a computer. Although brainware seems to be wired initially by nature, it has to change in some way in order to think and memorize. Antonym—Mindware. See Mind.

Bu gan wei tian xia xian (Chinese)—See Humility.

Bu shan (Chinese)—See Incompetent.

Buddha (c. 563-483 BC)—meaning the 'Enlightened One' was an Indian philosopher and founder of Buddhism.

Butterfly effect—associated with Lorenz's *Chaos Theory*. Although the universe might be a deterministic system, small differences in the initial conditions cause unpredictable outcomes or chaos. See Lorenz.

C

Chaos or disorder — part of the external reality that cannot be subjected to reason. It is associated with incomprehensibility, belief, predictability, unrecognizability, etc. The mind developed subconscious affectorial thinking to deal with the chaos of reality. Antonym—Order. See Lorenz and Second Law of Thermodynamics.

Chaos Theory—See Lorenz.

Charisma—ability to convince other people to follow without the followers questioning the reason to do so.

Chinese philosophers—Confucius, Lao Zi, Mencius, Ssu-ma Ch'ien, and Sun Zi).

Ching (Chinese)—See *Jing*.

Chu gou (Chinese)—See Straw dogs.

Chuan (Chinese)—See River.

Ci (Chinese)—See Compassion.

Clairvoyance—See Supernatural reality.

Clichés—See Aphorisms.

Closed system—system that neither affects external variables nor is affected by external variables. In other words, nothing gets in or out the system. Antonym—Open System. See System.

Cognitive—refers to thinking.

Cognitive dissonance—individual mental process rejecting correct information in order to protect the incorrect information that is already accepted by the subconscious of that individual as true. The reactive mindmode sends negative affecters to the conscious such as anxiety, frustration, and aggression to block the incoming information. Cognitive dissonance is unproductive for the individual, because it supports cognitive stagnation and failure. Cognitive dissonance can be expressed by aggression, agreeing to disagree, changing the topic, excessive talking, interrupting, passive silence, passive aggression, shouting, and violence. Antonym—Cognitive relevance. See Static thinking.

Cognitive irrelevance—new information does not fit into the information that we have already stored in our memory. It is like trying to fit a piece from one jigsaw puzzle into another one. Antonym—Cognitive relevance.

Cognitive relevance—new information fits into the information that we have already stored in our memory. It is like fitting a piece into the proper place of a jigsaw puzzle. Antonym—Cognitive irrelevance.

Collective—(1) mental nemonik referring to the collective mindmode. (2) An organized group of people with a common goal such as a family, business, tribe, nation, or the entire human race. (3) A description of the external reality that depends on the beliefs and perceptions of a particular group of people. See SCARRED, Collective mindmode, and Rational thinking.

Collective mindmode—way of rational thinking that generates artificial rules, which determine the rights and obligations of individuals within a collective and makes their behaviours predictable. Collective refers to an organized group of people with a common goal such as a family, business, tribe, nation, or the entire human race. Artificial refers to that part of the sensory reality that is manmade. The collective mindmode uses the mental order of reason to deal with the artificial order of the sensory reality. The Chinese philosopher Confucius was an important advocate of collective thinking. Collective specialists are found where proficiency in artificial rules is crucial such as in accountancy, bureaucracy, court, and government. Keywords for the collective mindmode include: artificial, artificial facts, artificial rules, bureaucracy, conflict, conform, control, cooperation, criminals, efficient, enforcement, hierarchy, indoctrination, inequality, judiciary, law and order, law-making, negotiation, obligations, outlaws, social perfection, privileges, punishment, rational thinking, rebellion, revolution, reward, suppression, verdicts, etc. See Rational thinking.

Collective specialists—operate where artificial rules are crucial such as in accountancy, bureaucracy, judiciary, and government. See Collective mindmode.

Collective thinking—See Collective mindmode.

Compassion (Chinese *cí*)—affectorial sympathy for other people that inhibits competitive behaviour in order to maximize the probability of success. Compassion is one of Lao Zi's three treasures. Compassion provides courage and strength. Compassion for other people prevents counterproductive harmonisations. See SCARRED.

Comperation—maximization of success by applying both natural competition and cooperation. To achieve success we have to use the most fitting strategy for each situation. The word 'comperation' indicates that competition and cooperation are complementary opposites. You cannot adequately compete without sufficient cooperation to maintain your strength. You cannot adequately co-operate without sufficient competition to remove your weaknesses.

Competence (Chinese *shan*)—See *De* (Chinese).

Competition—See Natural competition and Hyper-competition.

Complementary opposites—opposing polarities that cannot exist without each other. We can only perceive one by perceiving the other. There is no *Yin* without *Yang* and vice versa. There is no good without evil, no beauty without ugliness, no long without short, and no wealth without poverty. See LaoZi and *Dao De Jing*.

Comprehensive—See Exhaustive.

Computer programmer—See Programmer.

Conceal—projectional nemonik that prompts the mind to project false information to the sensory reality. Keywords for conceal include: ambush, avoid, camouflage, careful, cloak, confuse, covert, deceitful, disguise, dishonest, disinformation, front, insincere, dishonest, disloyal, distrust, false, hide, lying, mask, obscure, opponents, outgoing information, projection, screen, secret, strict criterion, trap, undercover, underground, untrue, etc. See Projection.

Concentration—intentional mental process that fosters conscious dominance by focusing consciously on a particular aspect of the sensory reality in order to inhibit unintentional conscious thoughts. Opposite—Relaxation. See Meditation, Nemonik meditation.

Concrete operational stage—See Piaget.

Confucian facts—See Artificial facts.

Confucian knowledge—See Artificial knowledge.

Confucian rules—See Artificial rules.

Confucian virtue—See Artificial virtue.

Confucian way—See Artificial way.

Confucius, Kung Ciu, or Kung Chung-ni (551-479 BC)—
Chinese philosopher who was one of the first to address
the problems concerning the artificial rules of the collec-
tives. He was a contemporary of Lao Zi. However, Lao
Zi's philosophy diametrically opposes the ideas of Confucius. Confucius elaborated on what Lao Zi calls The Way
of People (Chinese *Dè*). Lao Zi pointed out that The Way
of Nature (Chinese *Dao*) is always superior to The Way of
the People. After Confucius' death, his students compiled
his ideas in a manuscript called: The Analects. See Collective mindmode, *De*, Lao Zi, and *Dao De Jing*.

Conscious—small part of the mind that is only active when
that person is fully awake. The conscious is associated
with awareness, concentration, learning, sensory reality,
and rational thinking. Antonym—Subconscious. See
Mind and Rational thinking.

Conscious dominance—healthy mental state that is fostered
by concentration. During this state, the conscious is active, while the conscious awareness of subconscious activity is inhibited. The aim of this state includes learning new
tasks, providing direction, and managing the subconscious.
See Mind, Semiconscious dominance, and Subconscious
dominance.

Consistent arguments—feature a strong connection between
the facts. In the argument (A > B, B > C, therefore A >
C), (B is a common factor in the facts A > B and B > C).
See Logical argument.

Constant of the Cosmos—See Nothingness.

Constant of the Sages—Alignment with the Way (*Dao*). See LaoZi and *Dao De Jing*.

Constant of the Universe—See Harmonisation.

Constructed reality—See Internal reality.

Control—maintaining an imbalance between *Yin* and *Yang* that the Way (*Dao*) continuously seeks to harmonise. See LaoZi and *Dao De Jing*.

Conventional thinking—incomplete and unsystematic way of thinking that maximizes the probability of winning by applying a corrupted way of rational thinking propagated by the educational system. Rational thinking is a conscious way of thinking associated with logic and reason. Furthermore, conventional thinking contains convergent, creative, critical, deductive, divergent, dynamic, emotional, inductive, intuitive, lateral, linear, logical, rational, scientific, static, strategical, tactical, and vertical ways of thinking. Some of those methods are incomplete, ill-defined, and poorly understood. Conventional thinking lacks also a supporting theory and a model for the mind. Hence, conventional thinking is a loose collection of cognitive methods, rather than a coherent and systematic cognitive process. The prime aim of conventional thinking is maximizing the probability of winning. Winning is defeating opponents in competitions. By definition, winning is conflict oriented, which fosters aggression, enemies, and win-lose strategies. SCARRED is the acronym that represents the main weaknesses of conventional thinking. SCARRED stands for—**S**tatic, rather than dynamic thinking; **C**riticizing, rather than critical thinking; **A**nswering, rather than questioning; **R**ationalizing, rather than rational thinking; **R**ighteous, rather than collective; **E**ducated, rather than wise; **De**tached, rather than compassionate. Reality shows that humanity's conventional way of thinking is failing dramatically. As a result, we are facing global problems such as overpopulation, dwindling resources, domestic and industrial pollution, war, and climate change. We cannot solve those problems with the same way of thinking that has created them. Yesterday's solutions have created today's problems. Therefore, we need to upgrade to nemonik thinking. Antonym—Success. See Nemonik thinking.

Convergent thinking—way of thinking that aims to provide the only correct answer on a specific question. Convergence is the process of coming together. In this case, the specific question and the only answer. The term convergent thinking was coined by Joy Paul Guilford. Convergent thinking is incorporated in rational thinking. Antonym—Divergent thinking. See Conventional thinking and SCARRED.

Cooperation—See Natural cooperation and Hypercooperation.

Co-opetition—strategy that combines competition and cooperation in the business world. This combination of competition and co-operation creates a dynamic relationship. In business, you have simultaneously to compete and co-operate (Nalebuff and Brandenburger, 1996). See Comperation.

Copernicus, Nicolaus (1473-1543)—Polish astronomer who introduced the idea that the Earth orbits the Sun. See Scientist.

Cosmos—sum of Existence and Non-existence, matter and antimatter, or our Universe and any parallel or anti-Universe. See LaoZi and *Dao De Jing*.

Counterproductive harmonisations—harmonisations of the *Yin-Yang* balance by the Way (*Dao*) that threaten success.

Detrimental would be a subjective label, because all harmonisations are neutral. See Harmonisations, Beneficial
harmonisations, Lao Zi, and *Dao De Jing*.

Creation—"The One created the Two. The Two created the
Three. The Three created All-things" (Lao Zi). See First
division, Second division, Third division, Oneness, Two,
Three, All-things, *Dao*, Nothingness, Existence, Non-
existence, LaoZi, *Dao De Jing*, and Big Bang.

Creative—(1) mental nemonik that refers to the creative
mindmode. (2) A new description of reality. See Creative
mindmode.

Creative affecters—new descriptions of the chaos of reality,
which are generated by the creative mindmode. They include discoveries, fantasies, ideas, innovations, insights, inspirations, inventions, novelties, etc. Antonym—Reactive
affecters. See Creative mindmode.

Creative mindmode—way of affectorial thinking that deals
with the unknown or inexperienced aspects of reality by
generating creative affecters. Creative affecters include
discoveries, fantasies, ideas, innovations, insights, inspirations, inventions, novelties, etc. The seventeen nemoniks
are memory prompts and markers for mind mapping that
foster the associative processes of the creative mindmode.
The creative mindmode uses mental disorganisation or
chaos to deal with the chaos of reality. For example,
brainstorming is a random process that fosters creativity.
The creative mindmode provides new experiences and,
therefore, it moves people outside their comfort zone. Joy
Paul Guilford and Edward de Bono extended our
knowledge about creative thinking. Guilford introduced
'divergent thinking' and de Bono *'lateral thinking'*. Creative
specialists are found where originality is crucial such as in
art, design, invention, research, etc. Keywords for the cre-

ative mindmode include: art, conception, creative affecters, creativity, different, discoveries, , divergent thinking, exceptional, fantasy, hatching, ideas, incubation, inexperience, innovations, insights, inspirations, inventions, lateral thinking, new, novel, original, progress, questions, randomizing, unknown, etc. See Subconscious.

Creative specialists—operate where originality is crucial such as in art, design, invention, research, etc. See Creative mindmode.

Creative thinking—See Creative mindmode.

Creativity—See Creative mindmode.

Critical thinking—part of rational thinking that submits descriptions of reality to reason and logic in order to find the truth. Socrates developed a questioning version of critical thinking to discover the truth. Conventional thinkers such as politicians and lawyers replace critical thinking with criticizing to win debates independent of the truth. Critical thinking fosters emotional detachment. Antonym—Criticizing. See Rational thinking and SCARRED.

Criticizing—corrupted version of critical thinking that challenges descriptions of reality in order to win debates. Antonym—Critical thinking. See Conventional thinking and SCARRED.

CS7-virus—cognitive, self-protective, malignant, contagious, self-replicating, and epidemical virus that creates and maintains humanity's failing way of conventional thinking. CS stands for 'Cognitive Scars', while the number 7 refers to the seven cognitive scars that create and maintain conventional thinking. Those seven scars are represented by the previously explained acronym SCARRED. In accord, conventional thinkers are biased towards—staticism, criticism, answering, rationalization, righteousness, education, and detachment.

D

Da (Chinese)—See Greatnesses.

Da dao (Chinese)—See Great road.

Da jiang (Chinese)—See Master Carpenter.

da Vinci, Leonardo (1452-1519)—Italian Renaissance genius during the period of the High Renaissance. He excelled as an anatomist, architect, botanist, cartographer, engineer, geologist, inventor, mathematician, musician, painter, sculptor, and writer. His most famous painting is the Mona Lisa. See Scientists.

Da xiang (Chinese)—See Great Image.

Dao (Chinese)—means literally 'road, path, way, or pathway'. However, in the context of Lao Zi's philosophy, *Dao* means *The Way of Nature* or simply *The Way*. The Way is the core of Lau Tzu's philosophy and is the origin, principle, substance, and force of the Universe. Nowadays, we would call the study of the Way *Physics*. The Way explains the Universe, the meaning of life and our place in nature. The Way is the highest of Lao Zi's Four Greatnesses that constitute the Universe. The Way is constant, elusive, eternal, infinite, unstoppable, and neutral. It has so many manifestations that it cannot be given a single name. Although water can manifest itself as ice or steam, its true essence remains water. Similarly, the Way has different manifestations, but its true essence remains the Way. It may manifest itself as a soft rain on a summer afternoon, a spinning electron, lightening, a tornado, an earthquake, a waterfall, a supernova, a black hole and so on. Hence, Lao Zi uses many synonyms and metaphors to describe those manifestations of the Way. The Way of Lao Zi is based on the unchangeable rules of the Universe and is natural,

eternal, unchangeable, and objective. In contrast, the way
of Confucius is based on manmade rules and is artificial,
temporary, changeable, and subjective. Therefore, Lao
Zi's Way of Nature is of a higher order than the Confucian
Way of People. The Way is bound to maintain the cosmological constancy of Nothingness and, therefore, will always harmonise the *Yin-Yang* balance. The Way becomes
clearly detectable as the harmonising force (Chinese *qi*)
during the harmonisation of the *Yin-Yang* balance. After
each harmonisation, the Way will be undetectable again
and return to nothingness. *Dao* is a phonetic notation of a
Chinese pictograph and, therefore, it is alternatively
spelled as Tao. See LaoZi, and *Dao De Jing*.

Dao De Jing—book written by Lao Zi about two-and-half
thousand years ago. *Dao De Jing* means a classic (*Jing*)
about the Way of Nature (*Dao*) and the Way of People
(*De*). Nowadays, we call the Way of the Nature *Physics*,
while the Way of the people has become *Psychology*. Thus,
the modern meaning of *Dao De Jing* is: *A Classic about Physics and Psychology.* Lao Zi summarises succinctly the purpose of *Dao De Jing* with a quotation of the ancient sages:
"Use it to obtain what you seek and to escape what you suffer."
The title *Dao De Jing* is a phonetic notation of Chinese pictographs and, therefore, it is alternatively spelled as
DaoDeJing, Daodejing, Dao De Jing, TaoTeChing, Taoteching,
etc. See LaoZi.

DaoDeJing—See *Dao De Jing*.

Daodejing—See *Dao De Jing*.

Daoism—philosophical and religious system with millions of
followers that maintains that one should follow the rules
of nature, rather than the rules of the collective. For that
reason, one should empty the mind of all doctrines and
knowledge. In that way, one will return to the Oneness of

Dao and exceed all distinctions, even the one between life
and death. Some *Dao*ists consider Lao Zi to be a divine
person. However, Lao Zi's Four Greatnesses do not include the *Divine* and there is no indication in *Dao De Jing*
that Lao Zi saw himself as a divine being. See Lao Zi, and
Dao De Jing.

Dark-energy—force that counteracts the gravitational pull.
Researchers of the Supernova Cosmology Project at
Berkeley and the High-Z Supernova Search Team in Aus-
tralia discovered in 1998 that the expansion of the Universe is accelerating rather than decelerating. This effect
suggests the existence of a 'dark force' that counteracts the
gravitational pull (Leitl, 1999).

Darwin, Charles Robert (1809-1883)—proposed the theory
of natural selection. This theory holds that nature selects
organisms on inherited variations that increase their ability
to survive and reproduce.

De (Chinese)—means literally *virtue.* In the context of Lao
Zi's *Dao De Jing,* it means the Way of the People. Nowadays, we call studying the way of the people *Psychology.*
Furthermore, Lao Zi's concept of virtue diametrically opposes that of his contemporary Confucius. Whereas Lao
Zi's virtue is based on natural laws (objective mindmode),
Confucius' virtue is based on artificial rules (collective
mindmode). Hence, Laozian sages align with the Way of
Nature and foster natural virtue. Confucian sages align
with the Way of People and foster artificial virtue. *De* is a
phonetic notation of a Chinese pictograph and, therefore,
it is alternatively spelled as *Te.* Antonym—Artificial virtue.
See Lao Zi, and *Dao De Jing.*

de Bono, Edward (1933--)—Maltese consultant, inventor,
and physician who introduced lateral thinking in 1970.
Lateral thinking is a way of creative thinking that reformu-

lates problems and looks at them from different perspectives in order to find solutions. Furthermore, Edward de Bono advocates the inclusion of thinking in the school curriculum. Nemonik thinking providers the tools for lateral thinking. See Creative mindmode.

Debugging—finding and solving logical errors in a computer program or cognitive process.

Decision-making—the conscious might reason, but the subconscious will decide. The real decisions are made by the subconscious, while the conscious receives the decisions as affecters from the reactive mindmode. After that, the conscious might rationalize the decisions. The processes underlying decision-making are hidden in the subconscious. This suggests that it is impossible to develop an adequate rational theory about decision-making. Decisions are often judgment calls. See Prepare and Judgement-calls.

Deductive thinking—conscious way of thinking that derives a conclusion from one or more facts. For example, (Fact 1: All men are mortal) (Fact 2: Socrates is a man) (Conclusion: Socrates is mortal). More than two thousand years ago, the Greek philosophers Socrates, Plato, and Aristotle initiated the development of deductive thinking. Deductive thinking is incorporated in rational thinking. Antonym—inductive thinking. See Conventional thinking.

Deepening—using mantras to increase semiconscious dominance. See Nemonik meditation

Defragmentation—reorganizing separated information into united information. It is like organizing a random pile of books into a systematic library. After that organization, all the books about a particular topic are stored in the same place. Hence, defragmentation facilitates the efficient storage, maintenance, recall, and reorganization of information. The seventeen nemoniks of nemonik thinking will defragment the mind and memory and, therefore, increase the mental efficiency. See Memory.

Delusion - incorrect belief that is maintained in the face of contrasting reason. See Cognitive dissonance and Groupthink.

Democratis (c. 460-370 BC)—Greek philosopher who suggested that our reality comprised both Substance and Nothing. In his philosophy, atoms are the origin of all substances. See Greek philosophers.

Density—amount of energy wrapped up in a volume unit of matter. See Matter.

Desolate (Chinese *xiao*)—state of the Way (*Dao*) prior to the formation of the Universe. See LaoZi, and *Dao De Jing*.

Detachment—rationalized impartiality in regard to other people that fosters competitive behaviour in order to maximize the probability of winning. Antonym—Compassion. Conventional thinking and SCARRED.

Detection—process of perceiving sensory signals through the senses. See Perception.

Determinism—notion that future phenomena are fully determined by their initial conditions. Hence, in a deterministic reality, phenomena are predictable. Determinism is part of *Chaos Theory*. Determinism is based on the perceived order of the sensory reality. See Lorenz.

Detrimental harmonisations—See Counterproductive harmonisations.

Devil's advocate—literally an official who puts the case against the beatification or canonization. In daily life, the person who always defends the opposite or antithesis. See Groupthink and Nemonik accelerator.

Di (Chinese)—See Earth.

Dialectic—See Hegel.

Dialectic-accelerator—See Nemonik-accelerator.

Dirac, Paul (1902-1984)—predicted in 1928 the existence of antiparticles. The important discovery of the positron by Carl Anderson in 1932 confirmed his idea. A positron is an antiparticle that has the opposite electrical charge of an electron, which is a particle of ordinary matter. In 1955, Owen Chamberlain and Emilio Segrè discovered the anti-proton. This supports Lao Zi's idea that the Universe was created by dividing Nothingness in Existence (matter) and Non-existence (antimatter). See LaoZi, *Dao De Jing*.

Directional expansion—growth of a collective or individual towards a predetermined mission. Antonym—Non-directional expansion. See Expansion and Prepare.

Disorder—See Chaos.

Disorganizing or randomizing—process of transforming order into chaos. Antonym—Organizing.

Dispose—material nemonik that prompts the mind to decrease the amount matter that is under control. Keywords for dispose include: abandon, abolish, alienate, assassinate, banish, breakup, cast off, delete, demolish, depose, destroy, detach, disband, discard, discharge, discriminate, dismiss, dispel, disregard, divorce, eject, eliminate, eradicate, erase, exile, expel, exterminate, extinguish, let go, matter, moving on, obsolete, ostracise, outdated, purge, reduce, redundant, remove, separate, split, squander, terminate, waste, etc. See Matter.

Distortion—phenomenon in the internal reality that is not supported by the sensory reality, but maintained by the subconscious despite irrefutable evidence to the contrary. See Perception.

Divergent thinking—way of creative thinking that aims to provide multiple solutions for a single problem. Mental processes that move from details to the entirety. The term divergent thinking was coined by Joy Paul Guilford. Divergent thinking is the opposite of convergent thinking. Divergent thinking is incorporated in the creative mindmode of nemonik thinking. Antonym—Convergent thinking. See Creative mindmode and Conventional thinking.

Divine power—See Supernatural reality.

Dominance—See Conscious dominance, Semiconscious dominance, and Subconscious dominance.

Dominance window—hypothetical window that determines the mental state by sliding over the mental continuum, which ranges from conscious dominance to subconscious dominance. See Mind.

Dream awareness—conscious awareness of subconscious dreams that are inconsistent with the sensory reality and occur during semiconscious dominance. All people seem to dream. However, some are unaware of their dreams. See Dreaming.

Dreaming—subconscious process that updates the brain and mind with information that was collected during conscious dominance. See Dream awareness.

Dynamic balance—magnitudes of the particular entities change slowly over time, while the balance between their magnitudes is maintained. It is a balance in motion. We may compare it with a rubber balloon inflated with gas. If you slowly deflate the balloon then there is a dynamic balance between the contraction of the rubber and the pressure of the gas. That balance is continuously readjusted by the release of gas and is therefore dynamic. Although it is changing continuously, there is a balance at any given moment in time. Whenever you stop the gas from escaping, you create immediately a static balance between the contracting and expanding forces. The Sun is an example of a dynamic balance between nuclear and gravitational forces. Antonym—Static balance. See LaoZi and *Dao De Jing*.

Dynamic thinking—flexible and unbiased way of thinking that considers all nemoniks equally and applies the ones that fit the actual situation. Nemonik thinking is based on dynamic thinking. Hence, nemonik thinkers have no need to maintain the status quo by force. They just apply the nemoniks that provide the best fit to the actual situation. Hence, they adjust their thinking to the situation, like sailors who adjust their sails to the wind. Antonym—Static thinking. See Nemonik thinking, and SCARRED.

Dynamism—adapting to the Way of Nature (*Dao*), rather than trying to control or change the Way. A continuous process of harmonising of the *Yin-Yang* balance by the Way. The Way will gradually transform the dynamic *Yin-Yang* balance into a static balance. Hence, dynamism is temporary. Antonym—Stasis. See Dynamic thinking, LaoZi, and *Dao De Jing*.

Dyslexia—impairment in reading ability not resulting from low intelligence. See Affectorial thinking.

E

Earth (Chinese di)—third of the four Greatnesses that constitute the Universe. "The Way is Great; the Sky is Great; the Earth is Great; and the King is also Great" (Lao Zi). See LaoZi and Dao De Jing.

Educated—person who is in the possession of knowledge. See Education and SCARRED.

Education—mental process that transfers systematically detailed knowledge and skills from a teacher to a student. See Conventional thinking and SCARRED.

Efficiency—achieving success with a minimum of effort and resources. An effective person or collective will be efficient and is focused on the right mission. Doing the right things right. See Nemonik thinking.

Effort (Chinese shi)—strenuous and vigorous exertion to achieve success. In Lao Zi's philosophy, effort is a compass that shows you how to negotiate life's dangerous rapids. When you have to use effort to achieve success, you know that you are opposing the Way (Dao). See LaoZi and Dao De Jing.

Einstein, Albert (1879-1955)—Swiss scientist who published in 1905 three papers that revolutionized Newtonian physics. The papers addressed the electromagnetic radiation of light, special theory of relativity, and the idea that mass and energy are equivalent. Einstein formulated the theory of relativity, which holds that it is impossible to determine absolute motion. This theory did lead to the notion of a four-dimensional space-time continuum. At Princeton, Einstein attempted to unify the laws of physics. His well-known formula $E = mc^2$ shows the relationship between energy (E), mass (m) and the constant speed of light (c).

Given that the speed of light is 300,000 kilometres a second, c-squared is a very large number. Einstein's formula shows that infinitesimal amounts of matter contain immense amounts of energy. His formula shows also that energy is equivalent to matter and vice versa. This equivalence is in accord with Lao Zi's idea of Oneness. Furthermore, Einstein synthesized Newton's thesis that light comprised small particles with Young's antithesis that light was a wave. See Scientists.

Emotional flooding—conscious overload of reactive affecters. Affectorial thinking depends on subconscious mindsets. Hence, affectorial thinking requires an open communication between the conscious and subconscious. The subconscious is the seat of emotions and, therefore, opening the subconscious could overload the conscious with emotions. See Affectorial thinking.

Emotive thinking—subconscious way of thinking that convinces the conscious with emotions that a particular description of reality is either true or false regardless of the presented evidence. Emotive thinking is incorporated in the reactive mindmode of nemonik thinking. Antonym—Rational thinking. See Reactive mindmode.

Emptiness (Chinese *liao*)—state of the Way (*Dao*) prior to the formation of the Universe. See Lao Zi, and *Dao De Jing*.

Empty mind (Chinese *xu xin*)—See Silent mind.

Energy of the Universe (Chinese *qi*)—manifestation of *Dao* as *Qi* during the restoration of the *Yin-Yang* balance. See Lao Zi and *Dao De Jing*.

Enlightenment—discovery of the subconscious. See Affectorial thinking, Semiconscious dominance, Lao Zi, and *Dao De Jing*.

Entropy—decrease of order in a closed system. In simple words, things in the sensory reality will always decay. See Second Law of Thermodynamics.

EQ—Emotional Quotient, which provides insight in one's emotional intelligence. See IQ.

ESP (extrasensory perception)—See Supernatural reality.

Exhaustive—complete, all-inclusive, and comprehensive in reference to the mind, sensory reality, and their interaction. Nemonik thinking is an exhaustive way of thinking that includes all options. See Nemonik thinking and Nemonik template.

Existence (Chinese *you*)—everything that we can perceive in the sensory reality. Existence and Non-existence were created during the first division of the Way (*Dao*) in its manifestation of Nothingness or Oneness. Existence is the complementary opposite of Non-existence. Nothingness is the absence of both Existence and Non-existence. Neither Existence nor Non-existence can be nothingness on its own. They need each other to recreate Nothingness. See LaoZi, and *Dao De Jing*.

Expansion—See Advance and Accumulate.

External aids—conditioned stimuli in the sensory reality that foster semiconscious dominance. See Nemonik meditation.

EXTERNAL REALITY (DIAGRAM)

External Reality		
Sensory	Extrasensory	
	Scientific	Supernatural
known	unknown	unknowable
Internal Reality		

External reality—material and immaterial phenomena that
surround the mind. The external reality comprises the
sensory and extrasensory realities. The extrasensory reality
comprises the scientific and supernatural realities. The
subconscious creates the internal, constructed, or simulated reality from the external reality. See Extrasensory reality, Internal reality, Scientific reality, Senses, Sensory reality,
Sensors, and Supernatural reality. See diagram.

Extrasensory perception (ESP)—See Supernatural reality.

Extrasensory reality—part of the external reality that cannot
be perceived through the natural human senses. The extrasensory reality comprises the scientific and supernatural
realities. See External reality, Internal reality, Scientific reality, Senses, Sensory reality, Sensors, and Supernatural reality.

Extremes—disturbances of the *Yin-Yang* balance. Nothingness is the constant that cannot be changed and, therefore,
the Way will reduce both abundances and shortages. See
LaoZi and *Dao De Jing.*

F

Factoids—hypothesized bits of information that are stored subconsciously and are the basis for subconscious affectorial thinking. A bit is the smallest peace of information possible. To prevent conscious overload the processing of factoids is excluded from conscious awareness. See Affectorial thinking.

Facts—testable descriptions of reality that are supported adequately by sensory perception and reason. Facts can be divided into natural and artificial facts. Acquiring facts transforms chaos into order. Hence, the distinction between order and chaos depends on the development of one's mind, rather than on features of reality. Antonym—Belief. See Rational thinking.

False—description of reality that is inconsistent with the sensory reality. See Logical argument.

Fata morgana—See Mirage.

Father of the Multitude (Chinese *zhong fu*)—metaphor for the Way (*Dao*). See Lao Zi and *Dao De Jing*.

First division—division of Oneness or Nothingness (*Dao*) in the Two. Oneness or Nothingness is the manifestation of the Way (*Dao*) as the undivided void of desolate emptiness, while the Two are Existence and Non-existence. In terms of mathematics, the first division could be written as: $0 = (+1) + (-1)$. The first division might have been what scientists describe as the Big Bang. See First division, Second division, Third division, Oneness, Two, Three, All-things, *Dao*, Nothingness, Existence, Non-existence, LaoZi, *Dao De Jing*, and Big Bang.

First Law of Thermodynamics—introduced by Newton and is concerned with the conservation of energy. It states that energy cannot be destroyed or created. In addition, Einstein's formula $E = mc^2$ shows that matter and energy are interchangeable. That implies that the sum of matter and energy cannot be destroyed or created and is a constant. In Lao Zi's theory, Nothingness is the ultimate constant of the Cosmos. The sum of Existence and Non-existence is this unchangeable Nothingness. Hence, the total amount of matter and energy in the Existence cannot be increased or decreased without changing an equivalent in the inaccessible Non-existence. Otherwise, the constant of Nothingness itself would cease to exist, because it would have been changed into something. Hence, Lao Zi's theory implies a rationale for the observation mentioned in the first law that energy cannot be destroyed or created. See Newton, Second law, Third law, Lao Zi, and *Dao De Jing*.

Folk wisdoms—See Aphorisms.

Force—manifestation of the Way (*Dao*) as the unstoppable, neutral, and elusive power *Qi* that will harmonise each *Yin-Yang* balance. See *Qi*, LaoZi, and *Dao De Jing*.

Formal logic—part of reason that submits facts to validity rules in order to evaluate the truth of logical arguments and draw true conclusions, which become new facts. See Rational thinking.

Formal operational stage—See Piaget.

Four Greatnesses (Chinese *si da*)—Lao Zi proposes that there are four Greatnesses in the Universe, which are in descending order *The Way, Sky, Earth, and King*. The King is a symbol for the people. Some might argue that Lao Zi proposes five entities, with nature representing the highest one. However, the Way (*Dao*) and nature are the same. Lao Zi does not mention divine power as one of the four

Greatnesses. His Greatnesses are physical entities, rather than divine or spiritual ones. See LaoZi, and *Dao De Jing.*

Four stages of the formation: See Three stages of the formation.

Freud, Sigmund (1856-1939)—pioneer of Western psychology who introduced the psychoanalysis of the subconscious.

Frugality (Chinese *sè*)—economic moderation that avoids extreme spending or wasting resources. As they say Waste *not, want not!* Frugality is one of Lao Zi's three treasures. He points out that there can be no generosity without frugality. Frugality does apply to both material and human resources. See Three treasures, LaoZi, and *Dao De Jing.*

Funnel thinking—See convergent thinking.

G

Galileo (1564-1642)—Italian physicist and astronomer who initiated with Johannes Kepler a scientific revolution that fostered the work of Sir Isaac Newton. Galileo is famous for his struggle against the oppression of science by the Catholic Church. He was summoned to the Vatican by the Inquisition and was forced to repent his ideas. After more than 300 hundred years, a papal commission acknowledged the Vatican's error in 1992. See Groupthink.

Genius—most able part of the mind that is hidden in the subconscious. See Subconscious.

Goal—intended individual or collective achievement, which could be either a mission or a target. See Prepare.

God—See Supernatural reality.

Gravitational force—force of celestial bodies that draws objects toward their centre. Examples of gravitational force are weight, falling objects, and black holes. In terms of Lao Zi's philosophy, gravitational force might be the archetype of *Yin*. See LaoZi and *Dao De Jing*.

Gravitational-energy—archetype of *Yin*. See *Yan, Yin*, Lao Zi, and *Dao De Jing*.

Great Image (Chinese *da xiang*)—metaphor for the Way (*Dao*). See LaoZi and *Dao De Jing*.

Great Road (Chinese *da dao*)—metaphor for the Way (*Dao*). See LaoZi and *Dao De Jing*.

Greatnesses (Chinese *da*)—See Four Greatnesses, LaoZi and *Dao De Jing*.

Greed—accumulation for the sake of accumulation. As they say—*Some know the price of everything and the value of nothing.* Greed causes unnecessary material imbalances and, therefore, it is likely to evoke counterproductive social friction. See Accumulate.

Greek philosophers—Anaximander, Anaximenes, Aristotle, Democratis, Parmenides, Plato, Pythagoras, Socrates, Solon, Thales, and Xenophon.

Groupthink—collective mental process rejecting correct information in order to protect incorrect information that is already accepted by the collective as true. Team members will coerce each other to comply with the group doctrine. Tools of groupthink are social rewards, peer pressure, ostracizing, labelling, ridicule, and aggression. Each team needs a devil's advocate who rattles the cage and will make the team members think about their beliefs. This prevents that the team develops tunnel vision and that members conform to unrealistic ideas. Groupthink is unproductive for the collective, because it supports cognitive stagnation and failure. See Cognitive dissonance, Devil's advocate, Static thinking, and Reject.

Gu (Chinese)—See Ancients.

Guderian, Heinz Wilhelm (1888-1954)—German Panzer General who introduced the concept of Blitzkrieg. See Blitzkrieg.

Guilford, Joy Paul (1897-1987)—US psychologist who developed Guilford's cube and introduced the concepts of convergent and divergent thinking. See Creative mindmode.

Guo (Chinese)—See Universe.

H

Habituation — mental process that derives mindsets from repetitive actions and thoughts. Habituation turns ultimately every repetitive action or thought into a mindset. See Mindset.

Hallucination—non-sensory distortion of the internal reality associated with an imaginary external phenomenon. See Perception, Accept, Reject, Delusion, Illusion, Miracle, and Mirage.

Hard-drive—main memory device of a computer.

Harmonisation (Chinese *hé*)—automatic process of maintaining and restoring the *Yin-Yang* balance by the Way (*Dao*). The Way is bound to maintain the cosmological constancy of Nothingness and, therefore it has to harmonise the *Yin-Yang* balance. Harmonisation is the constant of the Universe. During the process of harmonisation, the Way is often detectable by our senses as *Qi*. After each harmonisation, the Way will be undetectable again and return to Nothingness. See Beneficial harmonisations, Counterproductive harmonisations, Restoring the *Yin-Yang* balance, Harmony, *Qi*, Stasis, Lao Zi, and *Dao De Jing*.

Harmony or tranquillity—temporary state of balance between *Yin* and *Yang* when the Way (*Dao*) is dormant. See Productive harmonisations, Counterproductive harmonisations, Restoring the *Yin-Yang* balance, Stasis, Lao Zi, and *Dao De Jing*.

Hate—acid that eats away the hater's soul. Antonym—Love.

He (Chinese)—See Harmonisation.

Hegel, Frederich (1770-1831)—German philosopher who introduced a dialectic describing the progress of knowledge. During the first stage, an opinion or thesis is challenged by a conflicting opinion or antithesis. This results in a mental conflict between the opponents. During the second stage, this conflict is resolved into an agreement between the opponents. This agreement is the synthesis between thesis and antithesis. The synthesis becomes the new thesis and the process repeats itself. Each new thesis provides an improvement over the previous one. See Nemonik accelerator.

Heuristics—See Aphorisms.

Hierarchy of the Universe—See Four Greatnesses.

Holistic thinking—way of thinking that is concerned with the entirety of a phenomenon. The danger is that holistic thinkers ignore too many details. Ultimately, they might know nothing about everything. Antonym—Convergent thinking. See Divergent thinking.

Humanity—See King.

Humility—"not daring to become the world's first" (Chinese *bu gan wei tian xia xian*) is mental moderation that avoids arrogance. Humility is a prerequisite for the ability to align with harmonisations of the Way (*Dao*) and one of Lao Zi three treasures. Humility is knowing and accepting our place, which is the lowest in the hierarchy of the Universe. Antonym—Arrogant. See Four Greatnesses, Three treasures, LaoZi and *Dao De Jing*.

Humphrey, Albert S. (1926-2005)—American business consultant who introduced the SWOT-analysis. See Nemonik thinking.

Hyper-competition—behaviour to acquire sustenance in the form of artificial valuables that exceeds a person's needs for a lifetime. Nature does not produce sustenance for hoarding. Hoarding is a self-fulfilling prophecy. It creates artificial shortages that justify even more hoarding. Hyper-competition is potentially destructive because it removes unnecessarily too much healthy strength from a system. Antonym—Hyper-cooperation.

Hyper-cooperation—cooperation that a collective bureaucracy forces on people with an increasing system of rules. Although these rules may force a person to cooperate, they cannot motivate that person to provide the highest quantity and quality possible. Hyper-cooperation is based upon the *right* of assistance in accordance to the rules. It is potentially destructive, because it maintains too much weakness in a collective. Antonym—Hyper-competition.

Hypnosis—mental process during which a hypnotist evokes a deep relaxation in a participant and then makes suggestions that change the internal reality of that participant. After completing the changes, the hypnotist voices suggestion to restore conscious dominance. The suggestions to change remain effective after the subject is woken up by the hypnotist. See Nemonik meditation.

Hypothesis—testable description of reality that is not subjected to reason yet. Hypotheses include assumptions, postulations, presumptions, tenets, theories, etc. Facts and beliefs differ from hypotheses. See Antithesis, Hegel, Scientific method, Synthesis, and Thesis.

I

Idealism—pursuit of ideals. See Ideals.

Ideals—individual and collective beliefs about *what ought to be*, rather than *what is*. Ideals are predominantly associated with the past or future. See Idealism.

Illusion—incorrect sensory perception of a phenomenon in the sensory reality that is maintained by the subconscious in the face of contrasting reason. See Perception, Accept, Reject, Delusion, Hallucination, Miracle, and Mirage.

Immortal Valley Spirit (Chinese *yu shen bu si*)—metaphor for the Way (*Dao*).

Incompetence (Chinese *bu shan*)—opposing the Way (*Dao*) and perishing as a result. People do not perish because they are evil, but because they are incompetent. See Aligning with the Way, LaoZi and *Dao De Jing*.

Incubation period virus—time between the initial exposure to that virus and the first appearance of its symptoms. The incubation period of the CS7-virus equals the duration required for the educational indoctrination of conventional thinking.

Indoctrination—See Social control.

Inductive thinking—conscious way of thinking that generalizes or extrapolates facts in order to reach a conclusion. It moves from multiple observations to a particular case. The resulting *'facts'* provide evidence, but no absolute proof for the conclusion. Statistical analyses are based on inductive thinking. They provide probabilities, rather than absolute truths. The opposite of inductive thinking is deductive thinking. Inductive thinking is incorporated in rational thinking. Antonym—Deductive thinking. See Conventional thinking.

Inferior virtue (Chinese *xia dé*)—synonym for artificial virtue.

Informal logic—part of reason that might be based on former formal logic that the reactive mindmode has transformed into mindsets. Those mindsets affect the conscious with affecters comprising aphorisms. The advantage is that informal logic is efficient and provides instantaneously a *'Best Fit'* to the situation. For example, we might meet Socrates and immediately conclude that he is mortal, without applying formal logic. The advantage of informal logic is simplicity and speed, which comes often at the cost of an imperfect fit to reality. Antonym—Formal logic. See Reactive mindmode.

Information management—ability to manage the perception and projection of information in order to maximize success. See Interaction.

Information overload—counterproductive awareness of processing consciously too much information. See Perception.

Inner team—imaginary team of nemonik experts comprising the stereotypes of a scientist, judge, inventor, and computer programmer. They represent respectively the objective, collective, creative, and reactive mindmodes. Visualizing the stereotypes will foster an internal dialogue and, therefore, fosters thinking. See Semiconscious.

Inorganic—lifeless matter such as iron, rock, and water. Antonym—Organic. See Matter.

Instrument or Organon—book comprising ideas of Aristotle, which were compiled by the Peripatetics. See Rational thinking.

Interaction—effect of the mind on reality and vice versa. Whatever you do affects reality, while reality affects you. Reality is like a mirror that reflects your behaviour, which is called '*karma*'. The exhaustive components of interaction are *perception* and *projection*. Information management controls the flow of incoming and outgoing information. See Nemonik thinking.

Interactive nemoniks—nemoniks that deal with the interaction between the mind and reality. The four interactive nemoniks are *accept, reject, reveal, and conceal*. See Nemoniks and Interaction.

Interception—ability to integrate the dimensions of space, time and matter that underlies our ability to catch and escape material objects.

Internal reality—subjective spatial, material, and temporal conscious perception of the external reality that is created by the subconscious. People perceive their internal reality as the true reality. However, the internal reality is subjective, because not everyone's perception and interpretation of the external reality is the same. Consequently, your internal reality might differ from the true external reality. See External reality, Extrasensory reality, Scientific reality, Senses, Sensory reality, Sensors, and Supernatural reality.

Intuition—reactive affecters that are created from information stored in the subconscious in order to protect the conscious from information overload. See Reactive mindmode.

Intuitive thinking—subconscious way of reactive thinking that convinces the conscious with reactive affecters that a particular description of reality is either true or false without providing the underlying reason. See Reactive mindmode, Lao Zi, and *Dao De Jing*.

Inventor—stereotype of nemonik thinking representing the creative mindmode in the nemonik inner team. See Inner team.

Invisible hand—See Adam Smith, Lao Zi, and *Dao De Jing*.

IQ—Intelligence Quotient, which provides allegedly insight in one's intelligence. See EQ.

Irrational—negative label to discredit non-rational or affectorial thinking. Antonym—Rational.

J

Jing (Chinese)—means literally *'classic'*. Therefore, *Dao De Jing* is a classic book in terms of the Chinese literature. *Jing* is a phonetic notation of a Chinese pictograph and, therefore, it is alternatively spelled as Ching. See LaoZi and *Dao De Jing*.

Judge—stereotype of nemonik thinking representing the collective mindmode in the nemonik inner team. See Inner team.

Judgement-calls—intuitive decisions about risk-avoidance and risk-taking without sufficient conscious information. See Prepare.

Justice (Chinese *yi*)—artificial Confucian virtue that maintains imbalances in the collective. As history shows, extreme imbalances in the distribution of wealth, status, privileges and power ultimately leads to violent social struggles. When this happens, the wealthy and powerful usually call for *'justice'* in order to protect the imbalances that advantage them. Their kind of justice often results in the maintenance of the status quo by increasing law and order. Under the pretence of stabilising the collective, the powerful use force to defend social inequalities. See Collective mindmode.

K

Karma—repayment of your actions. In Lao Zi's philosophy, the immutable Nothingness is divided during the First division in Existence and Non-existence. Nothingness cannot be changed and, therefore, Existence cannot change. Hence, the Way (*Dao*) in its manifestation of *Qi* is forced to harmonize all *Yin-Yang* balances. Consequently, if our actions disturb such a balance then *Qi* will restore that balance. See LaoZi and *Dao De Jing*.

King (Chinese *wang*)—lowest of the four Greatnesses that constitute the Universe. *"The Sky is great; the Earth is great; and the King is also great" (Lao Zi)*. The King is a symbol for the people, because Lao Zi replaces subsequently King (Chinese *wang*) with people (Chinese *ren*): *"People follow the Earth; the Earth follows the Sky" (Lao Zi)*. See Four Greatnesses, LaoZi, and *Dao De Jing*.

Knowledge (Chinese *zhi*)—information about the sensory and extrasensory realities. Confucian artificial knowledge is about manmade rules, customs, rituals, laws, and regulations. On the other hand, Lao Zi rejects that artificial knowledge and advocates natural knowledge. Nemonik thinking synthesizes the Laozian natural knowledge (objective) with the Confucian artificial knowledge (collective). It also incorporates beliefs (reactive). See LaoZi, *Dao De Jing*.

Known—See Spencer.

Koan—riddles used in Zen Buddhism, which have no rational solution. Each Koan forces Zen students to find nonrational solutions with subconscious Affectorial thinking. For example, a Zen master brings his hands together, while saying to a student *"This is the sound of two hands clapping. What is the sound of one hand clapping?"* The koan will

make us think again, about what we have taken for grant-
ed. This process of questioning our beliefs with a different way of thinking may provide new insight in the illusion
that we call reality. Koans are useful for nemonik thinking, because they foster subconscious affectorial thinking.
See Zen Buddhism, Affectorial thinking, Lao Zi, and *Dao
De Jing*.

Kung Chung-ni (Chinese)—See Confucius.

Kung Ciu (Chinese)—See Confucius.

L

Lao Tse—See Lao Zi.

Lao Tsu—See Lao Zi.

Lao Zi (570-490 BC)—Chinese sage and philosopher who wrote about two-and-half thousand years ago the book *Dao De Jing*. Lao Zi was the first philosopher who made a distinction between objective and collective thinking. *Dao* (The Way of Nature) refers to objective thinking, while *De* (The Way of People) refers to collective thinking. Lao Zi advocated natural virtue and rejected the Confucian artificial virtue. Lao Zi's real name might have been Li Ehr, who was a historian in the state Chu. However, scholars disagree about the personal details of Lao Zi. The name Lao Zi is a phonetic notation of Chinese pictographs. Therefore, it is alternatively spelled as LaoZi, Laozi, Lao Zi, LaoTzu, Laotzu, Lao Tsu, LaoTsu, Laotsu, Lao Tse, LaoTse, Laotse, etc. See First division, Second division, Third division, Oneness, Two, Three, All-things, *Dao*, Nothingness, Existence, Non-existence, and *Dao De Jing*.

LaoTse—See Lao Zi.

Laotse—See Lao Zi.

LaoTsu—See Lao Zi.

Laotsu—See Lao Zi.

LaoTzu—See Lao Zi.

Laotzu—See Lao Zi.

LaoZi—See Lao Zi.

Laozi—See Lao Zi.

Laozian knowledge—See Natural knowledge.

Laozian virtue—See *De* (Chinese).

Laozian Way—See *Dao* (Chinese).

Lateral thinking—way of creative thinking that reformulates problems and looks at them from different perspectives in order to find solutions. Edward de Bono introduced this way of thinking in his book '*Lateral Thinking*' *(1970)*. The opposite of lateral thinking is vertical or rational thinking. Lateral thinking is part of the creative mindmode of nemonik thinking. However, nemonik thinking is superior, because it provides an exhaustive prompting system for de Bono's lateral thinking. Nemonik thinking is exhaustive and, therefore, the seventeen nemoniks provide all the possible perspectives to reformulate the actual problem. Each nemonik prompts the creative mindmode to generate questions and ideas from a different point of view. Hence, the nemonik template is a questions and ideas generator that adds process and structure to lateral thinking. Antonym—Vertical thinking. See Conventional thinking, Creative mindmode, de Bono, and Nemonik thinking.

Lax decision criterion—criterion that will accept information easily. The advantage of a lax decision criterion is that you accept most of the true information. Antonym—Strict decision criterion. See Accept.

Leaders—people who determine their own goals, take full authority and responsibility, create productive conditions, and convince others to support their goals. See Prepare.

Leonardo da Vince—See da Vinci.

Li (Chinese)—See Propriety.

Li Ehr (Chinese)—See Lao Zi.

Liang (Chinese)—See Two.

Liao (Chinese)—See Emptiness.

Linear thinking—systematic, directive, and step-by-step way of thinking that inhibits diversions and follows a predetermined narrow path to solve a problem. Linear thinking is incorporated in rational thinking. See Conventional thinking.

Listening—process of perceiving audio information. See Active listening.

Logic—See Logical thinking.

Logical argument—part of formal logic that contains a set of facts leading to an irrefutable conclusion that becomes a new fact. See Logical thinking.

Logical thinking—part of rational thinking that uses critical thinking, deductive thinking, inductive thinking, formal logic, and informal logic in order to test the truth of descriptions of reality. See Formal logic and Informal logic.

Lorenz, Edward (1917-2008)—American mathematician and meteorologist who, in 1963, introduced *Chaos Theory*, which holds that the universe is a deterministic chaos. Although the universe might be a deterministic system, small differences in the initial conditions cause unpredictable outcomes or chaos. Lorenz called this the butterfly effect. The notion that reality contains deterministic order and chaos raises the question how the mind deals with those aspects of reality. In nemonik thinking, the conscious deals with the order of reality, while the larger subconscious deals with the chaos of reality. See Mind, Determinism, and Sensory reality.

Love—"Those who live might lose their life. Those who do not love will never live." Antonym—Hate.

M

Ma Wang Dui (Chinese)—tomb of a nobleman at Ma Wang Dui in Chang Sha, south-central China. Dating from 168 BC and unearthed in 1973, the tomb contained two copies of Lao Zi's *Dao De Jing* that are now known as the Ma Wang Dui texts A and B. The tomb acted as a time-capsule and revealed crucial information about the true meaning of *Dao De Jing*. Ma Wang Dui is a phonetic notation of Chinese pictographs and, therefore, it is alternatively spelled as Mawangdui, Ma Wang tui, or Mawangtui. See Lao Zi and *Dao De Jing*.

Main mental bias—preference for either rational or affectorial thinking. See Mind.

Maintaining the *Yin-Yang* balance—preventing that either *Yin* or *Yang* becomes so large that the imbalance evokes a natural harmonisation. Maintaining the *Yin-Yang* balance is the first of the three fundamental alignments with the Way (*Dao*). The unstoppable Way, in its manifestation of *Qi*, will always harmonise the *Yin-Yang* balance, because it has to maintain the cosmological constancy of Nothingness. Therefore, sages will maintain the *Yin-Yang* balances, because it is a waste of time and effort to disturb them. See Aligning with harmonisations, Restoring the *Yin-Yang* balance, Lao Zi, and *Dao De Jing*.

Malthus, Thomas (1766-1834)—introduced a theory of population growth, which holds that the population increases faster than the food supply. Malthus' idea is supported by recent history. Although our technology has increased substantially the food production during the last century, this abundance did not prevent famine. Instead, the global population increased dramatically and famine is one of our main global problems.

Managers—people who are responsible for their personal performance and that of their team. See Specialists.

Mantra—repeated voiced or unvoiced phrase, word, or sound that fosters semiconscious dominance by inhibiting unintentional conscious thoughts. See Nemonik meditation.

Maslow, Abraham (1908-1970)—introduced the hierarchy of needs. From bottom to top: Physiological, Safety and security, Belonging and love, Esteem, and Self-actualisation. See Progress.

Mass-energy—archetype of *Yang*. See *Yin, Yang*, Lao Zi, and *Dao De Jing*.

Master Carpenter (Chinese *da jiang*)—metaphor for the Way (*Dao*).

Material—refers to matter.

Matter—three-dimensional finite part of reality that features substance, volume, and weight, and occupies and moves through space and time. Matter is wrapped up energy that is determined by four features: density, volume, shape, and motion. Matter is part of the sensory reality. Matter is organic or inorganic and includes resources such as animals, energy, equipment, information, money, people, plants, raw materials, etc. Einstein's formula $E = mc^2$ shows that energy (E) is another manifestation of matter (m). Information is classified as matter, because there is no information without matter. Matter provides the exhaustive options to *Accumulate, Preserve, and Dispose*. Transformation is a combination of accumulation and disposing matter. Antonym—Antimatter. See Sensory reality.

Meditation—intentional mental process that fosters concentration on relaxation. Meditation fosters semiconscious dominance by focusing consciously on a particular aspect of the internal reality, which inhibits unintentional conscious thoughts. A person in meditation maintains continuously a delicate balance between conscious and subconscious dominance. See Mind (Diagram), Concentration, Relaxation, Hypnosis, and Nemonik meditation.

Memory—self-organising and associative mental process that stores, maintains, and recalls information in order to preserve it across space and time. Nemoniks, defragmentation, and prompting are tools to improve the memory. See Mind.

Mencius (c. 372-289 BC)—Chinese Confucian philosopher.

Mental—refers to the mind.

Mental accelerator—See Nemonik-accelerator.

Mental bias—cognitive distortion that is caused by a consistent preference for a specific way of thinking. As the Universe is dynamic, any mental bias will sooner or later become counterproductive. See Static thinking.

Mental disorganization—used by the creative mindmode to generate creative affecters by unfreezing, disorganizing, reorganizing, and refreezing the memorized information. Hence, the creative mindmode uses mental disorganisation or chaos to deal with the chaos of reality. Mental disorganisation is a hypothesized mental process, because it is hidden in the subconscious. See Creative mindmode.

Mental immune system—subconscious mental system that protects the information that is already accepted by the mind as correct. However, that protection becomes malignant when the mind protects incorrect information. The mental immune system uses cognitive dissonance and groupthink.

Mental irrelevance—See Cognitive irrelevance.

Mental manipulation—mental processes such as analysing, integrating, reorganizing and interpreting information.

Mental nemoniks—nemoniks that refer to a particular mind-mode. They are the *objective, collective, creative, and reactive mindmode.* See Nemonik thinking.

Mental Non-action—See Non-action and Silent mind.

Mental overload—See Information overload.

Mental processes—processes of the mind such as thinking, memory, contemplation, awareness, emotions, feelings, creativity, reason, intuition, sense perception, conception, judgment and understanding. See Mind.

Mental reconstruction—subconscious reconstruction of the objective sensory reality into the conscious subjective internal reality.

Mental relevance—See Cognitive relevance.

Mental state—distinct level of awareness such as conscious dominance, subconscious dominance, semiconscious dominance, and unconsciousness.

Mental structures—relatively permanent parts of the mind such as the conscious, semiconscious, and subconscious.

Meta-analysis—analysis that summarises the results from earlier studies in order to draw conclusions from their results.

Meta-thinking—thinking about the way we think. Hence, studying nemonik thinking is a way of meta-thinking. See Psychology.

Notes

Mind—nonmaterial part of a person that comprises the total of all conscious, subconscious, and semiconscious mental structures and processes. The mind is abstract and can only exist in the extrasensory reality, because you cannot see, hear, taste, smell, or touch the mind. The mind is a theoretical construct that exists paradoxically in the mind. Nevertheless, this elusive construct helps us to evaluate our way of thinking. A healthy mind has a will, purpose, or intent that maintains goals such as maximizing success, obtaining comfort, escaping discomfort, and sustaining survival. Furthermore, it has abilities to think and memorize, and to maintain a productive interaction with the external reality. The mind has to deal with the order and chaos of reality. Therefore, the mind generates respectively rational thinking and affectorial thinking. Rational thinking is divided in the objective and collective mindmodes, while affectorial thinking is divided in the creative and reactive mindmodes. Concentration fosters conscious dominance and rational thinking. On the other hand, relaxation fosters subconscious dominance and affectorial thinking. See Affectorial thinking, Brainware, Concentration, Conscious, Diagram of the mind, Meditation, Memory, Mindmode, Mindware, Nemonik thinking, Rational thinking, Semiconscious, Subconscious, and Thinking. See diagram.

Mind management—conscious management of the subconscious mind. Mind managements targets pain, emotions, motivation, attitude, emergency responses, intuitions, gut feelings etc. See Nemonik meditation.

Mind map—diagram showing the relationship between concepts that fosters understanding.

MIND (DIAGRAM)

Diagram of the Mind

Conscious	Semiconscious	Subconscious
Concentration	Meditation	relaxation
Rational thinking		Affectorial thinking
Objective — Collective		Creative — Reactive

Mind, body and spirit—holistic entity that cannot be split without losing some of its characteristics. The precise divisions between mind body and spirit are still unclear, because none of these entities can be studied in isolation. The mind and spirit cannot be studied directly, because they are nonmaterial.

Mindmode—specific way of thinking that deals with a specific aspect of the external reality. They comprise the *objective, collective, creative, and reactive mindmodes*. Each mindmode is an elementary way of thinking that has evolved as a result of natural environmental pressure. They are defined by different interactions between the order and chaos of the mental process versus the order and chaos of reality. (1) The objective mindmode uses mental order to deal with the natural order of reality. (2) The collective mindmode uses mental order to deal with the artificial order of reality. (3) The creative mindmode uses mental disorganization or chaos to deal with the chaos of reality. (4) The reactive mindmode uses mental order to deal with the chaos of reality. See Collective mindmode, Creative mindmode, Mind, Nemonik thinking, Objective mindmode, and Reactive mindmode.

Mindmode-analysis—evaluates the exhaustive interactions of the four mental nemoniks with the thirteen operational nemoniks in order to find the nemoniks that provide the *Best Fit* to the actual situation. See Nemonik thinking.

Mindsets—internalized sets of rules that are derived by the reactive mindmode from the past, the known, or experience in order to generate reactive affecters. Initially, mindsets are created by your conscious and stored in your subconscious. Every repetitive action or thought becomes ultimately a mindset. The reactive mindmode generates mindsets through the process of habituation. In computer science, mindsets could be compared to algorithms. The aim of mindsets is to increase our speed and accuracy of our decisions and actions by using pre-programmed instructions. The application of mindsets requires subconscious dominance or a silent mind. The mindsets are honed each time they are used. After each improvement, there is less need for conscious interference and the mindset sinks deeper into our subconscious. A disadvantage is the rigidity of the action or thoughts evoked by a mindset. See Reactive mindmode.

Mindware—hypothetical set of nonmaterial self-organizing processes that creates and maintains the mind. Mindware could be compared to the software of a computer. Mindware is learned and, therefore, the nurtured component of thinking. Mindware is supported by brainware. Antonym—Brainware. See Mind.

Ming (Chinese)—See Named.

Minkowski, Hermann (1864-1909)—Professor at the Zurich Federal Institute of Technology and Einstein's tutor. He proclaimed that Einstein never bothered about mathematics and called him a *'lazy dog'*. Apparently, Minkowski was a rational thinker who did not appreciate Einstein's affectorial way of thinking. Minkowski introduced a geometrical version of the special theory of relativity. See Scientists.

Miracles—supernatural phenomena that defy the laws of nature. That could be floating rocks, ghostly apparitions, revelations about the future, speaking marble statues, etc. See Perception, Delusion, Hallucination, Illusion, and Mirage.

Mirage or fata morgana—optical illusion that might be perceived by many people as real, but it is caused by atmospheric conditions. See Perception, Delusion, Hallucination, Illusion, and Miracle.

Mission—long-term or ultimate goal of a person or collective. My mission is to help people to become the best thinkers they can be. See Goal.

Mission effectiveness—ability of a person or collective to accomplish its mission. Mission effectiveness is doing the right things right at the right time. See Mission, Mission statement, Efficiency and Effectiveness.

Mission statement—comprises the rationale for the actions of a person or group. It sets the group or person apart from other groups or persons. For example, my mission statement is to help people to become the best thinkers they can be. See Mission effectiveness.

Mnemonic—Greek word meaning memory aid. See Nemonik.

Model of the mind—diagram that shows the important components of the mind and their main interactions. The nemonik model of the mind includes the conscious, subconscious, and semiconscious. It features the conscious objective and collective mindmodes, and the subconscious creative and reactive mindmodes. See Diagram of the mind, and Nemonik thinking.

Moderation (Chinese *wu ji*)—avoiding extreme values of either *Yin* or *Yang*. See LaoZi and *Dao De Jing*.

Mother (Chinese *mu*)—metaphor for the Way (*Dao*). See LaoZi and *Dao De Jing*.

Motivation—mental drive to maximize success. See Reactive mindmode.

Mottos—See Aphorisms.

Mu (Chinese)—See Mother.

Mysterious Female (Chinese *xuan pin*)—metaphor for the
Way (*Dao*).

N

Named (Chinese *ming*)—divided manifestation of the Way (*Dao*). See LaoZi and *Dao De Jing*.

Nameless (Chinese *wu ming*)—undivided manifestation of the Way as the Oneness or Simplicity. See LaoZi and *Dao De Jing*.

Nameless Simplicity (Chinese *wu ming pu*)—undivided manifestation of the Way (*Dao*) as Oneness. See LaoZi and *Dao De Jing*.

Naming or Being Named (Chinese *you ming*)—process of dividing entities in parts. After something is divided into smaller parts, we need names in order to differentiate these parts from each other. In Lao Zi's philosophy, naming is the illusionary division of the Way (*Dao*). The division of the Way is illusionary, because the Way is the Oneness, which cannot really be divided. Lao Zi's idea is similar to ideas in quantum mechanics. See LaoZi and *Dao De Jing*.

Napoleon Bonaparte—See Bonaparte.

Natural—refers to that part of reality that is not manmade. Antonym—Artificial. See Objective mindmode.

Natural competition—behaviour to acquire sustenance for one year.

Natural cooperation—entirely voluntarily cooperation. Voluntary or natural cooperation fosters mutual dependency, gratitude, and friendship. See Collective mindmode.

Natural facts—unchangeable facts about nature. See Objective mindmode.

Natural knowledge—knowledge about the laws of nature or the laws of physics. Natural knowledge is objective, unchangeable, and eternal. It is the knowledge of scientists and of Lao Zi. The laws of nature were always there and will always be there. We may discover and rediscover them, but we cannot change them. Nemonik thinking incorporates Natural knowledge (objective). See Objective mindmode, Scientist, LaoZi, and *Dao De Jing*.

Natural laws—objective descriptions of the unchangeable cause-effect relationships of nature or the laws of physics. See *Dao De Jing*, LaoZi, Objective mindmode, and Scientists.

Natural virtue (Chinese *zhi de*)—competence to align with the Way of nature *(Dao)*. It is the competence to be in the right place, at the right time, with the right resources, and in the right frame of mind. The Way is objective and eternal. Therefore, virtue that is based upon the Way is also objective and eternal. The unstoppable Way is the highest Greatness in the hierarchy of the Universe. Hence, natural virtue or Laozian virtue (objective) is superior to artificial or Confucian virtue, which is based on temporary manmade rules. See LaoZi and *Dao De Jing*.

Natural Way—See *Dao* (Chinese).

Nemonik-accelerator—cognitive method that increases the speed of your thinking by fostering agreement during disagreement, while fostering disagreement during agreement. This tool is based on Hegel's dialectic. See Hegel and Nemonik thinking.

NEMONIK THINKING (DIAGRAM)

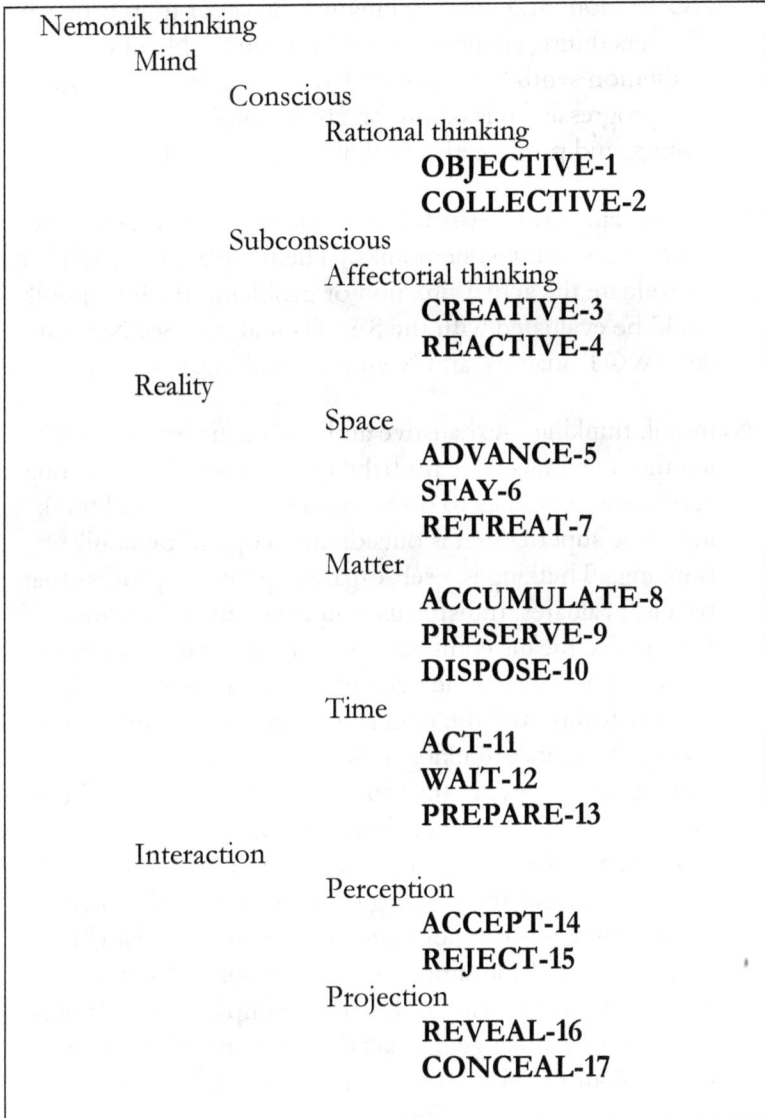

Nemonik thinking
   Mind
      Conscious
         Rational thinking
            OBJECTIVE-1
            COLLECTIVE-2
      Subconscious
         Affectorial thinking
            CREATIVE-3
            REACTIVE-4
   Reality
         Space
            ADVANCE-5
            STAY-6
            RETREAT-7
         Matter
            ACCUMULATE-8
            PRESERVE-9
            DISPOSE-10
         Time
            ACT-11
            WAIT-12
            PREPARE-13
   Interaction
         Perception
            ACCEPT-14
            REJECT-15
         Projection
            REVEAL-16
            CONCEAL-17

Nemonik meditation—special type of meditation that uses visualizations and unvoiced mantras in order to improve affecters during semiconscious dominance. Nemonik meditation synthesizes auto-balance, visualizations, mantras, progressive relaxation, breathing management, conditioning, and positive affirmations. See Meditation.

Nemonik template—basis for nemonik thinking, which comprises the seventeen nemoniks. The template is a checklist to evaluate the actual situation or problem. Each nemonik could be evaluated with the SWOT-analysis. See Nemoniks, SWOT-analysis, and Nemonik thinking.

Nemonik thinking—exhaustive and systematic way of thinking that maximizes the probability of success by subjecting seventeen nemoniks to both rational and affectorial thinking. The supernatural is outside the scope of nemonik thinking. Thinking is a self-organizing mental process that recalls, evaluates, transforms, and generates information. Exhaustive means complete, all-inclusive, comprehensive, and every possibility included in reference to the mind, sensory reality, and the interaction between the mind and reality. Nemonik thinking is dynamic because it adjusts efficiently to changes in the sensory reality. Nemonik thinking is systematic and, therefore, it is the first teachable way of thinking. Rational thinking is a conscious way of thinking that is associated with logic and reason. Affectorial thinking is a subconscious way of thinking associated with creativity, beliefs, intuitions, and emotions.—Nemonik thinking is unique, easy to learn and simple to use. It mobilizes your hidden genius, accelerates your thinking, improves your memory, reveals opportunities and threats, creates questions and ideas, and reduces your stress levels.—The prime aim of nemonik thinking is maximizing the probability of success. *Success is to obtain what you seek and escape what you suffer (Lao Zi).* Life is relatively fair, because you will get most of the time exactly what you ask for. If you ask for nothing, then you are likely to get nothing. Incompetent thinkers ask for the wrong things and set the wrong goals. Therefore, they obtain only what they suffer most and escape what they need most. This shows that Lao Zi's idea of success is *goal oriented*. Lao Zi's definition of success does not require you to defeat opponents in competitions, and therefore, it fosters compassion, allies, and win-win strategies. In contrast, conventional thinking is an incomplete, static, and unsystematic way of thinking, which is propagated by the educational system. It maximizes the probability of winning by applying a corrupted way of rational thinking. The prime aim of conventional thinking is maximizing the probability of winning. Winning is defeating opponents in competitions. Winning is by definition *conflict oriented*, which fosters aggression, enemies, and win-lose strategies. Therefore, goal oriented nemonik thinking is more productive than conflict oriented conventional thinking.—To add wisdom to the system of nemonik thinking, it incorporates ideas from Sun Zi's book *The Art of War*, Lao Zi's *Dao De Jing*, and Baltasar Gracián's *The Art of Worldly Wisdom*. Nemonik thinkers also use an inner team, which is an imagined team of four cognitive experts. Furthermore, nemonik thinkers are unpredictable because they follow Lao Zi's advice— *Competent strategists have no strategy*. Nemonik thinkers create strategies and tactics that fit the particular situation.— Nemonik thinking is to conventional thinking what algebra is to simple arithmetic. You can do things with algebra that are almost impossible with simple arithmetic. In the same way, you can do things with nemonik thinking that are almost impossible with conventional thinking. However, nemonik thinking is much easier than algebra because it is based on common sense. Nemonik thinking is neutral, and therefore, you can apply nemonik thinking independent of your age, education, gender, ideology, profession, race, religion, or socio-economic background.— Nemonik thinking applies to every aspect of life including art, business, conflict resolution, economics, politics, relationships, science, technology, warfare, etc. Nemonik thinking will foster your goals, whether you are a teacher or student, industrialist or environmentalist, or warrior or peacemaker.—Nemonik thinking is balanced because it relies equally on the reason of the head and the passion of the heart. It is fast because it produces instantaneously strategic templates that take optimal advantage of the situation at hand. This helps you to think on your feet in emergencies. Nevertheless, nemonik thinking is not a cure for mental illnesses. For such problems, seek advice of a healthcare professional.—Conventional thinking is time consuming. Hence, the less time you have, the greater your necessity to study this manual. Nemonik thinking is crucial because it deploys your full mental potential. You might be the smartest thinker in the world, but only nemonik thinking can make you the smartest thinker you can be. All it takes is 17 words! See Conventional thinking and SCARRED.

Nemoniks—memorized keywords describing the exhaustive aspects of the mind, reality, and the interaction of the mind and reality, which prompt the memory to recall associated information. The word nemonik is a phonetic notation of the Greek word mnemonic, which means *memory aid*. In accord, nemoniks improve your thinking by defragmenting your memory and prompting your memory to recall information. However, nemoniks are more than plain mnemonics. Nemoniks are also mental tools for guiding your thinking, consciously managing your larger subconscious, activating your subconscious to generate ideas and reveal intuitions, and building tactics and strategies. Furthermore, the constant readiness of the nemoniks is expected to reduce your anxiety and stress levels. Furthermore, the four mental nemoniks include the *objective, collective, creative, and the reactive mindmodes*. The nine reality nemoniks include *advance, stay, retreat, accumulate, preserve, dis-*

pose, act, wait, and prepare. The four interactive nemoniks include *accept, reject, reveal, and conceal.* The thirteen operational nemoniks include the nine reality nemoniks and four interactive nemoniks. Best of all, you do not have to worry nemonik thinking, because the nemoniks will be habituated automatically by your subconscious. Ultimately, nemonik thinking is like playing a musical keyboard with seventeen keys producing an infinite repertoire of strategies to deal with the sensory reality. See Nemonik thinking. See Nemonik template.

Nerve signals—uniform electrical-chemical signals carrying coded information about the sensory reality from the senses to the brain. See Brainware.

Networking—skill to foster personal relationships in order to maximize success. See Prepare and Organizing.

New Age—broad philosophical and spiritual movement, which was inspired by the approach of this era and focuses on the holistic entity of the mind, body, and spirit in order to improve interpersonal relations by expanding human awareness. See Mind, body, and spirit.

Newton, Sir Isaac (1642-1727)—British mathematician and physicists who described in his book *Principia* some of the basic laws of nature. Einstein synthesized Newton's thesis that light comprised small particles with Young's antithesis that light was a wave. See First Law of Thermodynamics, Second Law of Thermodynamics, Third Law of Motion, and Scientists.

Newton's Third Law of Motion—See Third Law of Motion.

Non-action (Chinese *wu wei*)—means literally action *'without action'*. The principle of Non-action entails an efficient use of the unlimited force of the Way so that sages achieve their goals with a minimum of effort and resources. It does not mean that sages are lazy, passive, or fatalistic. Sages have to be alert and time their actions to align themselves with the Way. For instance, one could travel in leisure by using sails, rather than using depleting one's strength with rowing. See LaoZi and *Dao De Jing*.

Non-directional expansion or organic expansion—growth of a collective towards available opportunities without having a predetermined mission. Antonym—Directional expansion. See Expansion and Prepare.

Non-existence (Chinese *wu*)—cannot be perceived and is diametrically opposed to Existence. Non-existence and Existence were created during the first division of the Way (*Dao*) in its manifestation of Nothingness. Existence is the complementary opposite of Non-existence. Nothingness is the absence of both Existence and Non-existence. Neither Existence nor Non-existence can be nothingness on its own. They need each other to recreate Nothingness. Lao Zi's concept of Non-existence is not just the absence of existence. It is less than nothing—it is a shortage of existence. Lao Zi's idea of Non-existence might be similar to the modern idea of antimatter. Antonym—Existence. See First division, Second division, Third division, Oneness, Two, Three, All-things, *Dao*, Nothingness, Existence, LaoZi, and *Dao De Jing*.

Non-rational thinking—negative label to discredit non-rational or affectorial thinking. See Affectorial thinking.

Non-thinking—affectorial thinking that is subconscious thinking without conscious thinking. Antonym—Rational thinking. See Affectorial thinking, Silent mind, LaoZi, and *Dao De Jing*.

Normal—collective judgement that a person's internal reality is within the collectively accepted perception of the external reality. Antonym—Normal. See Collective mind-mode.

Nothing—concept of early Greek philosophy that means the empty space in our reality. This has nothing to do with Lao Zi's notion of Nothingness, which is the origin of the Universe. See Nothingness, LaoZi, and *Dao De Jing*.

Nothingness—manifestation of the Way (*Dao*) as the undivided void of desolate emptiness that was the origin of the Universe. Nothingness is devoid of substance and is ultimately inconceivable. Nothingness is the true constant of the Cosmos that cannot be decreased or increased. During the first division, Nothingness was divided into Non-existence and Existence. Nothingness is the sum and absence of both Existence and Non-existence. See First division, Second division, Third division, Oneness, Two, Three, All-things, *Dao*, Existence, Non-existence, LaoZi, and *Dao De Jing*.

Nova—sudden increase in the brightness of a star that gradually fades. See Nuclear force.

Nuclear force—pertains to the nucleus or core of matter. Einstein showed with his formula $E = mc^2$ the immense amounts of nuclear energy in matter. In nature, nuclear energy is evident in the radiation of the Sun and from supernovas, while it is used by humanity in nuclear power plants and nuclear weapons. In terms of Lao Zi's philosophy, nuclear force is the archetype of *Yang*. See Einstein, *Yang*, LaoZi, and *Dao De Jing*.

O

Objective—(1) mental nemonik that refers to the objective mindmode. (2) Description of reality that is independent of what anyone believes. See Nemoniks and Objective mindmode.

Objective mindmode—way of rational thinking that deals with the natural order of the sensory reality, which can be described by natural laws and facts that make nature predictable. Objective refers to a description of reality that is independent of what anyone believes. The objective mindmode is a conscious way of thinking that is activated by concentration.—In contrast to the collective mindmode, the objective mindmode pertains to the laws of nature. In contrast to the creative mindmode, the objective mindmode will increase our knowledge step-by-step in an incremental way.—The objective mindmode uses the mental order of reason to deal with the natural order of reality. Objective thinking generates science. Sir Isaac Newton was the one of the first scientists to describe objectively the laws of the sensory reality. Albert Einstein and Max Planck extended Newton's ideas into the extrasensory reality. Objective specialists are found where proficiency in natural laws is crucial such as in science and technology. Keywords for the objective mindmode include: data collection, experimentation, formal logic, hypothesis tests, literature reviews, mathematics, measurements, natural facts, natural laws, natural, rational thinking, reliability tests, replicated results, samples, science, scientific method, sensory observations, statistical analyses, testing, truth, validity tests, etc. See Aristotle, Concentration, Conscious dominance, Logic, Mind, Order, Natural knowledge, Rational thinking, Reason, Science, and Sensory reality.

Objective specialists—found where proficiency in natural laws is crucial such as in science and technology. See Objective and Objective mindmode.

One—See Oneness.

Oneness (Chinese *yi*)—manifestation of the Way (*Dao*) as the indivisible or nameless entity that comprises our Existence. See First division, Second division, Third division, Two, Three, All-things, *Dao*, Nothingness, Existence, Non-existence, LaoZi, and *Dao De Jing*.

Open system—affects external variables or is affected by them. In other words, things can get in and out of the system. Antonym—Closed system. See System.

Operating system—basic software that tells a set of electronic components how to act as a computer. Similarly, nemonik thinking is the operating system for the brain. It tells the brain how to act as a thinker. Hence, nemonik thinking is for the brain what Windows is for the computer. Antonym—Mindware. See Nemonik thinking.

Operational bias—mental distortion that is caused by a consistent preference for a specific operational nemonik. See Operational Nemoniks.

Operational nemoniks—thirteen nemoniks comprising the nine reality nemoniks and the four interactive nemoniks. See Nemoniks.

Operations—See Rational-operations.

Opportunity—potential advantage. For example, receiving a job offer is an opportunity. An opportunity is optional and the outcome depends on the decision of the person. Antonym—Threat. See SWOT analysis.

Order—part of the external reality that can be subjected to reason. It is associated with comprehensibility, knowledge, predictability, recognisability, etc. The mind developed conscious rational thinking to deal with the order of reality. Antonym—Chaos. See Rational thinking and Second Law of Thermodynamics.

Organic—refers to matter that is alive such as animals, microbes, plants, and people. Antonym—Inorganic. See Matter.

Organic expansion—See Non-directional expansion.

Organizing—process of transforming chaos into order. Organizing is the allocation, integration, and movement of mental, spatial, material, temporal, and interactive resources into a unified system that is ready to carry out a plan. Organizing requires skills such as negotiation, promoting, and networking. Antonym—Disorganizing. See Creative mindmode.

Organon—See Instrument.

Origin of the Universe—See *Dao* and Nothingness. LaoZi and *Dao De Jing*.

Overload—See Information overload.

P

Panic—counterproductive conflict between the conscious and subconscious for mental dominance that paralysis the mind. See Reactive mindmode and Rashness.

Parallel universe—See anti-universe. See LaoZi and *Dao De Jing.*

Paranormal—See Supernatural reality.

Parapsychological (PSI)—See Supernatural reality.

Para-sensory—See Supernatural reality.

Parmenides (c. 510-450 BC)—Greek philosopher who suggested that Nothing could not exist and that all substances were eternal. This idea has a similarity with quantum mechanics. In accord with Lao Zi's philosophy, Nothingness was divided in Existence and Non-existence. In our sensory reality of Existence, there is no Nothingness. See Greek philosophers, First division, Nothingness, LaoZi, and *Dao De Jing.*

Peers—people who have a similar socio-economic background in common.

People—See King, LaoZi, and *Dao De Jing.*

Perception—part of the nemonik interaction that manages the incoming information flow from the sensory reality towards the mind. The senses facilitate sensory perception by detecting incoming information. The exhaustive options provided by perception for maximizing success are to *Accept and Reject* information. Listening is an easy way to gain information. Antonym—Projection. See Interaction.

Perfection—ability to maximize one's efficiency, speed, and accuracy in order to adjust to the changes in reality. As the sensory reality changes continuously, perfection is a process, rather than a state. Perfection is driven by the urge to survive. See Prepare.

Perseverance—persistent continuation of a course of action despite difficulties and obstacles. See Reactive mindmode.

Peter's principle—people will be promoted to their level of incompetence. A person who is doing a great job is most likely to be promoted. Promotions stop when that person fails in the higher job. Hence, ultimately, all employees will occupy jobs they cannot handle. That is counterproductive for both the individual and the team. See Prepare.

Philosopher—means literally a lover of wisdom. See Philosophy.

Philosophy—the pursuit of wisdom that is obtained by means of reasoning rather than by experimentation or faith. Philosophy is about general causes, principles and the human perception of reality.

Physical Non-action—See Non-action.

Physics—study of the laws of nature. See LaoZi and *Dao De Jing*.

Piaget, Jean (1896-1980)—Swiss psychologist who described the four stages of cognitive development in children i.e. *sensorimotor, preoperational, concrete operational and formal operational*. Sensorimotor: at about two years of age, children have learned *'object permanence'*. They know that objects continue to exist even when they cannot be perceived anymore. At this age, children have also acquired a rudimentary language. Preoperational: at about seven years of age, children have learned the concept of *'conservation'*. They know that changing the shape of matter does not change the amount of that matter. Concrete operational: at about twelve years of age, children become capable of logical thought. Operational: children over twelve years of age have learned to think in abstract terms and think about past and future.

Ping Fa—See The Art of War.

Pingfa—See The Art of War.

Placebo—physiological inactive treatment such as a fake medication e.g. sugar pills. However, a working placebo is a psychological treatment that shows the working of the mind. See Reactive mindmode.

Plan—mental or physical map describing the intended actions across time required to reach a predetermined goal. Plans include strategies and tactics. See Prepare.

Planck, Max (1858-1947)—German theoretical physicist who introduced in 1900 quantum mechanics, which is concerned with infinitesimal subatomic phenomena outside the sensory reality, which are called quanta. See Scientists.

Planning—comprehensive examination of the spatial, material, temporal, perceptive, and projective aspects of the situation with the four mindmodes in order to create a plan. See Plan and Prepare.

Plato (427-347 BC)—Greek philosopher, student of Socrates and teacher of Aristotle. Plato was born in Athens and had a great influence on Western philosophy. He founded the Academy, which provided subjects such as astronomy, biology, mathematics, political theory, and philosophy. In Plato's writings, ideas were advanced, discussed, and criticized in the context of conversations. The core of his philosophy is his theory of forms or ideas. He proposed that knowledge must be certain and infallible. Reality is fixed, permanent, and unchanging. It is associated with 'Being' rather than 'Becoming'. Plato proposed that knowledge should be based on reason, rather than sense experience. In Plato's philosophy, the soul comprised the rational element, the will, and the appetites. The rational element and the will should control the appetites. Plato believed that immorality is the result of ignorance. He described the island Atlantis in the two dialogues *Timaeus and Critias*. See Greek philosophers.

Positioning—ability to manoeuvre into a situation where the strategic advantage is so large that the opposition has to avoid a conflict at all cost. Sun Zi warns against rash actions: *'Competent generals do not fight'*. Any conflict will destroy resources on both sides. Therefore, a superior general positions his army into a situation where the strategical advantage is so large that his opponent will avoid a battle. In that way, the general uses resources more effectively, prevent mutual destruction, minimise negative feelings and acquire new resources that are not damaged by conflict. See *The Art of War*, Prepare, and Sun Zi.

Positive affirmation—mantra that improves the subconscious e.g.—*Each day I feel better*. See Deepening, Hypnosis, Mantra, Meditation, Nemonik meditation, Progressive relaxation, and Relaxation.

Precognition—See Supernatural reality.

Predisposition—natural latent talent, which does not necessarily have to include an overt manifestation of that talent.

Preoperational stage—See Piaget.

Prepare—temporal nemonik that prompts the mind to get ready for action. Preparation includes analysing, decision-making, learning, mind management, negotiating, organizing, planning, positioning, prioritizing, risk-management, fostering leadership, setting goals, internalizing nemonik thinking, time management, training, etc. Preparation is productive if it is based on proactivity, while it is counterproductive if it is used as an excuse for procrastination. The 80/20 rule supports the notion that perfect preparation is counterproductive. Even imperfect things and actions might be extremely useful. Keywords for prepare include: analysing, decision-making, fostering leadership, internalizing nemonik thinking, learning, marketing, mind management, negotiating, organizing, planning, positioning, prioritizing, promotion, risk-management, setting goals, time, time-management, training, etc. See Nemoniks, Nemonik thinking, and Time.

Present—infinitesimal moment between the past and future that moves into the future with the speed of time. See Time.

Preserve—material nemonik that prompts the mind to maintain the same amount of matter that is under control. Keywords for preserve include: care, conserve, custody, contain, defend, depot, fortify, hold, keep, look after, maintain, matter, protect, retain, reserve, safeguard, save, secure, shelter, spare, stock, store, sustain, tend, etc. See Nemoniks, Nemonik thinking, and Matter.

Primordial substance—originating principle or single material element from which all other substances have evolved. Primordial substance is a concept used by the ancient Greek philosophers. This is comparable to Lao Zi's idea of the Way (*Dao*) in its manifestation of Nothingness. See Greek Philosophers, Nothingness, LaoZi, and *Dao De Jing*.

Principle of the Universe—the Way (*Dao*), in its manifestation of *Qi*, will always harmonise the *Yin-Yang* balance, because it has to maintain the cosmological constancy of Nothingness. See LaoZi, and *Dao De Jing*.

Priority—task that is so urgent or important that it has to be completed before any other task. See Prepare.

Proactivity—productive early action that fosters opportunities and inhibits threats. See Act and Wait.

Problem solving—nemonik thinking is a problem solving tool. It uses the nemonik checklist to raise questions, create ideas, identifying problems, strengths, weaknesses, opportunities, and threats. See Nemonik thinking and SWOT.

Procrastination—counterproductive delay of action that inhibits opportunities and fosters threats. See Act and Wait.

Productive harmonisations—harmonisations of the *Yin-Yang* balance by the Way (*Dao*) that foster success. Beneficial would be a subjective label, because all harmonisations are neutral. We conceive them only as being either counterproductive or productive in relation to our personal success. See Harmonisations, Lao Zi, and *Dao De Jing*.

Programmer—stereotype of nemonik thinking representing the reactive mindmode in the nemonik inner team. See Inner team.

Progress—process that decreases the distance to the goal or alternatively, increases the distance from the edge of survival. In our era, progress is defined often as the advance of science and the application of increasingly advanced technologies. See Advance.

Progressive relaxation—systematic and step-by-step process of alternating tension and relaxation of muscles. Progressive relaxation was introduced by Edmund Jacobson

(1888-1983). See Deepening, Hypnosis, Mantra, Positive affirmation, Meditation, Nemonik meditation, and Relaxation.

Projection—part of interaction that refers to managing the outgoing information flow from the mind towards the sensory reality. The exhaustive options provided by projection for maximizing success are to *Reveal and Conceal* information. Antonym—Perception. See Interaction.

Prompting—using a memorized phrase or word (prompt) to recall associated information from the memory. See Nemoniks and Memory.

Propriety (Chinese *li*)—artificial Confucian virtue that entails conformity to the system of rules and beliefs that maintain a society. Propriety tells us the way that things should and ought to be done. Propriety explains with collective arguments why it is proper to have socio-economic differences in the collective. Propriety is so deeply hidden in the soul that only young rebels (unconditioned) dare question its validity. See Collective mindmode, LaoZi, and *Dao De Jing*.

Proverbs—See Aphorisms.

PSI (parapsychological)—See Supernatural reality.

Psychokinesis—See Supernatural reality.

Psychologists—See de Bono, Freud, Guilford, and Piaget.

Psychology—study of the mind and behaviour. See *De*.

Pu (Chinese)—See Simplicity.

Pythagoras (c. 580-500 BC)—Greek philosopher who suggested that ultimately numbers were the physical origin of
all substances. See Greek philosophers.

Q

Qi or vital energy—manifestation of the Way (*Dao*) as the neutral force that will always harmonise the *Yin-Yang* balance in order to maintain the constant Nothingness. *Qi* is elusive and can hide in matter. It is only detectable when it restores the *Yin-Yang* balance. The energy of *Qi* is vital for all life, but it is neither good nor evil. See *Dao*, Nothingness, LaoZi, and *Dao De Jing*.

Questioning—See SCARRED.

R

Randomizing—See Disorganizing.

RAM—Randomly Accessible Memory of a computer.

Rapid-Eye-Movement—See REM sleep.

Rashness—fast but counterproductive decisions without adequate conscious thoughts or subconscious mindsets. Rashness stops the conflict between the conscious and subconscious for mental dominance, because the dice are thrown. Hence, rashness is often a counterproductive attempt to avoid or stop a panic attack. See Panic attack and Reactive mindmode.

Rational bias—consistent preference for rational thinking that is independent of the sensory reality. See Rational thinking.

Rational deadlock—prolonged dispute in which the opponents fail to reach an agreement, because they are unable to synthesize the thesis and antithesis. Therefore, they cannot proceed to the new thesis. Any deadlock will inhibit mental progress. A historic example was the scientific debate about the characteristics of light. A more recent example might become the debate about global warming versus global cooling. See Groupthink, cognitive dissonance, Rational thinking, and Hegel.

Rational thinking—conscious part of nemonik thinking that deals with the predictable order of reality by submitting facts to reason in order to create new facts. Rational thinking uses the mental order of reason to deal with the order of the sensory reality. The mental processes underlying rational thinking are within the conscious awareness, and therefore, they can be observed directly. Rational thinking comprises critical thinking that fosters distrust and emotional detachment. Concentration fosters conscious dominance and rational thinking. Rational thinking comprises the objective and collective mindmodes. Keywords for rational thinking include: alert, analyses, awake, cause-effect, concentration, conscious, consistent, constant, critical, detached, dispassionate, distrust, evidence, facts, impartial, impassive, logic, order, peer review, predictable, rationalization, reality-check, reason, systematic, truth, unbiased, unemotional, unprejudiced, etc. In Lao Zi's philosophy, rational thinking could be called *Yang* thinking. Antonym—Affectorial thinking. See Aristotle, Artificial knowledge, Collective mindmode, Concentration, Conscious, Law, Logic, Mind, Objective mindmode, Order, Rationalizing, Reason, SCARRED, Science, Sensory reality, and *Yang*.

Rationalizing—corrupted version of rational thinking that provides semi-rational justifications to defend a previously made conclusion. See Conventional thinking and SCARRED.

Rational-operations—part of rational thinking that comprises mental processes such as analysing, integrating, reorganizing, and interpreting. See Rational thinking.

Reactive—(1) mental nemonik referring to the reactive mindmode. (2) Mental or physical response without conscious thinking that is initiated by the reactive mindmode. See Reactive mindmode.

Reactive affecters—affecters that are generated by mindsets and deal with the chaos of reality. They include beliefs, common sense, desires, emotions, feelings, habits, heuristics, impulses, intuitions, reactions, reflexes, routines, sensibilities, skills, etc. See Affectorial thinking, Empty mind, Nemoniks, Reactive, Reactive mindmode, and Reactive specialists.

Reactive mindmode—way of affectorial thinking that deals with the chaos of reality by habituating mindsets that generate reactive affecters. Reactive affecters include beliefs, common sense, desires, emotions, habits, heuristics, impulses, informal logic, intuitions, reactions, reflexes, routines, sensibility, skills, etc. The reactive mindmode uses mental preparation or order to deal with the chaos of reality. It is the aim of the reactive mindmode to optimize your mental and physical perfection. However, the reactive mindmode is a product of the past. It relies on your experience and, therefore, it keeps you within your comfort zone. The Chinese philosopher Lao Zi advocated reactive thinking. Reactive specialists are found where individual perfection is crucial such as in chess, driving, martial arts, sports, surgery, etc. Keywords for the reactive mindmode include: accurate, belief, biased, common sense, confidence, desires, efficient, emergency, emotions, sensibility, experience, faith, gut-feeling, habituation, heuristics, hunch, impulses, individual perfection, informal logic, instinct, intuition, mindsets, motivation, order, passion, predictable, rash, reactions, reactive affecters, reflexes, routines, skills, speed, stability, traits, etc. See Affecters, Affectorial thinking, Chaos, Empty mind, External reality, Hypnosis, Meditation, Mind, Mindsets, Nemoniks, Positive affirmations, Reactive, Reactive specialists, Semiconscious dominance, Subconscious, and *Yin*.

Reactive specialists—found where individual perfection is crucial such as in chess, driving, martial arts, sports, surgery, etc. See Reactive mindmode.

Reality—See External reality.

Reality nemoniks—nemoniks that deal with the aspects of the sensory reality. The nine reality nemoniks are—*advance, stay, retreat, accumulate, preserve, dispose, act, wait, and prepare.* However, a complete strategy will comprise decisions about all seventeen nemoniks. See Nemoniks.

Reality-check—critical evaluation with rational thinking whether a particular affecter fits the sensory reality. It is a threat that the reality-check could become a rationalization for that affecter. See Rational thinking.

Reason—part of rational thinking that comprises formal logic and informal logic. See Aristotle.

Recreation—conscious replacement of activities that are essential for success with nonessential activities.

Reductionism—reducing the number of variables in order to reduce the chaos of the external reality. The danger is that reductionists lose contact with the sensory reality of everyday life. See Rational thinking and Sensory reality.

Reject—perceptual nemonik that prompts the mind to refuse the incoming information as a true description of the sensory reality. Keywords for reject include: careful, disaccord, disagree, disapprove, disbelieve, discontent, distrust, excluding, false, incoming information, incorrect, perception, rebellion, strict criterion, unconventional, unconvinced, untrue, etc. See Perception.

Relaxation—mental process that fosters subconscious dominance by inhibiting involuntary conscious thoughts. Opposite—Concentration. See Meditation, Nemonik meditation, and Progressive relaxation.

Reliability—refers to the accuracy of measurement. See Validity.

Reliable arguments—comprise only facts. In the argument (A > B, B > C, therefore A > C), (A should be indeed larger than B, while B should be indeed larger than C). See Logical argument.

Religion—institution that promotes the belief in a divine power, which is regarded to be the creator and leader of the universe. Most religions aim to describe the unknowable. See Reactive mindmode and Spencer.

REM sleep—stage of sleep characterized by rapid-eye-movements and dreaming, which occupies about twenty per cent of the sleeping time. See Subconscious.

Ren (Chinese)—See Benevolence.

Ren (Chinese)—See People.

Residual imbalances—unintentional imbalances of *Yin* and *Yang* that are remains of the intentional imbalances that technocrats created in order to achieve their goals. Although the Way (*Dao*), in its manifestation of *Qi*, will always harmonise the *Yin-Yang* balance, it may take very long before an artificially evoked imbalance is totally removed. See LaoZi and *Dao De Jing*.

Restoring the *Yin-Yang* balance—artificial process of restoring the *Yin-Yang* balance by people in order to defuse natural but counterproductive harmonisations by the Way (*Dao*). It is the third of the three fundamental alignments with the Way. The crucial imbalances in our environment that are caused by *Yang* technology and rational or *Yang* thinking demonstrate the importance of this fundamental alignment. We may have to defuse the potentially counterproductive harmonisations before they gain more momentum. Industrial pollution is a prime example. See Aligning with harmonisations, Maintaining the *Yin-Yang* balance, Harmonisation, Harmony, Stasis, LaoZi, and *Dao De Jing.*

Retreat—spatial nemonik that prompts the mind to increase the distance to the goal. Keywords for retreat include: abandon, apologize, backward, concede, constrict, defeated, depart, desert, disengage, dissociate, divorce, escape, evacuate, exit, exodus, fall back, flight, leave, pull back, recede, recoil, regress, resign, retire, retract, return, reverse, rout, setback, shrink, space, stampede, turn around, vacate, withdraw, etc. See Space, Nemoniks, and Nemonik thinking.

Reveal—projectional nemonik that prompts the mind to project true information to the sensory reality. Keywords for reveal include: allies, careless, confident, disclose, divulge, explain, explicit, expose, honest, lax criterion, projection, open, outgoing information, manifest, overt, plain, publish, slip, tell, trust, warning, etc. See Projection.

Righteous and Harmonious Fist—See Boxers.

Righteous thinking—corrupted version of collective thinking that creates rights without obligations for privileged individuals within a collective. This notion created a generation obsessed with entitlement. See Conventional thinking and SCARRED.

Risk-management—process of evaluating, comparing, and controlling the potential advantages and disadvantages of an action in order to maximize the probability of success. Risk-management is a sort of balancing act. Generally, high payouts are associated with high risks. It is like sailing a boat—if you do not take the risk of capsizing then you are unlikely to win the race. However, if you do take a high risk then might fail completely. Hence, there is a fine line between success and failure, and that line is determined by risk-management. See Prepare.

River (Chinese *chuan*)—metaphor for the Way (*Dao*).

Rules of thumb—See Aphorisms.

S

Sages (Chinese *sheng ren*)—wise people who align with the Natural Way (*Dao*) by fostering natural virtue (*Dè*). They are in the right place, at the right time, with the right resources and in the right frame of mind. On the other hand, Confucian sages align with the Artificial Way of the People by fostering artificial virtues. The term sage may refer to man and woman alike. See Natural virtue, Artificial virtue, Ancients, LaoZi, *Dao De Jing*, and Confucius.

San (Chinese)—See Three.

San bao (Chinese)—See Three treasures.

SCARRED—nemonik acronym that represents the seven main weaknesses of conventional thinking. **S**tatic, rather than dynamic thinking; **C**riticizing, rather than critical thinking; **A**nswering, rather than questioning; **R**ationalizing, rather than rational thinking; **R**ighteous, rather than collective; **E**ducated, rather than wise; **De**tached, rather than compassionate. See Conventional thinking.

Science—body of valid and reliable descriptions concerning the external reality.

Scientific Art of Living—applying scientific knowledge about nature to maximize success. Lao Zi summarizes in one line the purpose of this art: *"Use it (Dao) to obtain what you seek and to escape what you suffer."* See LaoZi and *Dao De Jing*.

Scientific method—process based on analysis, experimentation, data collection, formal logic, generalization, mathematics, measurements, natural laws, literature reviews, samples, sensory observations, peer review, theorizing, reason, reliability tests, replicated results, statistical analyses, hypotheses tests, validity tests, etc. The scientific method has supported the industrial, biotech, and informational revolutions. See Objective mindmode.

Scientific reality—part of the extrasensory reality that can be perceived with artificial sensors or rational thinking. See External reality, Extrasensory reality, Internal reality, Senses, Sensory reality, Sensors, and Supernatural reality.

Scientific reduction—reduction from the extrasensory reality to the scientific reality that is caused by the limitation of current knowledge.

Scientific thinking—See Objective mindmode.

Scientist—stereotype of a nemonik thinker representing the objective mindmode in the nemonik inner team. Famous scientists were Leonardo da Vinci, Nicolaus Copernicus, Sir Isaac Newton, Thomas Young, Hermann Minkowski, Albert Einstein, and Max Planck. See Objective thinking and Inner team.

Scorched earth—military strategy to destroy everything during a retreat, so that the opponent cannot use those resources. See Sun Zi and Strategy.

Se (Chinese)—See Frugality.

Second division—formation of the Universe as the result of the interaction between Existence and Non-Existence, which creates the Three Greatnesses. The Three Greatnesses are: The Sky, the Earth, and the King or the People. Subsequently, these Three Greatnesses generate All-things that are the myriad of organic and non-organic things in our Universe. See First division, Third division, Oneness, Two, Three, All-things, *Dao*, Nothingness, Existence, Non-existence, LaoZi, and *Dao De Jing*.

Second Law of Thermodynamics—entropy or chaos will always increase in a closed system, or alternatively, the order of a closed system will always decrease. In simple words, things will always decay. Order will be always transformed into chaos. This is an important law because it predicts that the future of our entire Universe will be ultimately a state of chaos. In contrast, Lao Zi's philosophy implies that the Universe is moving towards harmony. However, the difference might be in the definition of chaos. See First law, Third law, Order, Chaos, System, Open system, Closed system, LaoZi, and *Dao De Jing*.

Self—observer of a person's internal reality, which that person consciously calls 'I'. The Self of a healthy person is projected to the sensory reality through a set of relatively stable behavioural and mental characteristics. The essence of the Self is elusive because it tends to disappear when one tries to study it. Nevertheless, it is holistic because it is appears in every part of the mind. See Mind and Reactive mindmode.

Semiconscious—part of the mind that comprises parts of the conscious and subconscious, which form a communication channel between those parts of the mind. The semiconscious is associated with dream awareness, meditation, hypnosis, and drowsiness. See Mind.

Semiconscious dominance—healthy mental state that is fostered by meditation. This state fosters conscious awareness of subconscious activity and the conscious improvement of the subconscious way of affectorial thinking. See Conscious dominance, Semiconscious, and Subconscious dominance.

Sensations—subconsciously created phenomena in the internal reality that are derived from phenomena in the sensory reality.

Senses—integrated physiological and mental systems that perceive material signals from the sensory reality and transform them into neural signals. The five traditional senses are hearing, seeing, smelling, tasting, and touching. However, people have also senses for balance, body position, movement, pain, pressure, temperature, etc. See Sensors, Sensory reality, and Perception.

Sensorimotor stage—See Piaget.

Sensors—cells in the body that are able to detect sensory signals from the sensory reality and convert them into nerve signals. See Senses.

Sensory perception—perception by the senses of material signals that are emitted by the sensory reality. See Perception, Senses, and Sensory reality.

Sensory reality—part of the external reality that can be perceived directly through the natural human senses. If not otherwise indicated, *reality* means *sensory reality*. Lorenz emphasized the difference between the deterministic order and chaotic parts of reality. However, acquiring facts transforms chaos into order. Hence, the distinction between order and chaos depends on the development of one's mind, rather than on the features of the external reality. Therefore, that distinction is subjective, rather than objective. Organizing and disorganizing transform reality. The mind has developed different ways to deal with the order of reality (consciously) and chaos of reality (subconsciously). See External reality, Extrasensory reality, Internal reality, Scientific reality, Senses, Sensors, and Supernatural reality.

Sensory reduction—reduction from the external reality to the sensory reality, which is caused by the natural limitations

nemonik-thinking.org

of the human senses. See Senses, Sensory reality, and Perception.

Sensory signals—emitted or reflected by material objects within the sensory reality that can be detected by the senses. Sensory signals include pressure, heat, vibration, light, particles, etc. See Senses, Sensory reality, and Perception.

Shan (Chinese)—Competence. See Virtue.

Shang de (Chinese)—See Superior virtue.

Sheng ren (Chinese)—See Sages.

Shi (Chinese)—See Effort.

Shih Chi (Chinese)—Historical Records. See Ssu-ma Ch'ien.

Shui (Chinese)—See Water.

Shun dao (Chinese)—See Aligning with the Way.

Shun qi (Chinese)—See Aligning with harmonisations.

Si da (Chinese)—See Four Greatnesses.

Silent mind—mental state that is devoid of conscious thoughts and fosters subconscious action without conscious interference. A silent mind does not mean ignorance. A silent mind is the state of the mind when it is pure, tranquil, and at rest. The silent mind is also called the empty mind or the zone. However, the mind is silent, rather than empty. Relaxation, recreation, and meditation foster a silent mind. See Nemonik meditation.

Simplicity (Chinese *pu*)—synonym for the Way (*Dao*). It is the undivided manifestation of the Way as Oneness or

Nameless that is often called the uncarved or wooden block. See Oneness, LaoZi, and *Dao De Jing.*

Simulated reality—See Internal reality.

Sky (Chinese *tian*)—second of the Four Greatnesses that constitute the Universe. *"The Way is Great; the Sky is Great; the Earth is Great; and the King is also Great" (Lao Zi).* See Four Greatnesses, LaoZi, and *Dao De Jing.*

Sliding—mental process of shifting consciously the dominance window across the mental continuum. See Nemonik meditation.

Smith, Adam (1723-1790)—father of modern economy. In his famous treatise *The Wealth of Nations* (1776), he proposed that governments should adhere to the principle of free competition and should not interfere with the economy (laissez-faire). He suggested that the production and exchange of goods could only improve through free competition. Individuals serve the common good best when they pursue their own interest. This free competition would create an *'invisible hand'* which would regulate the economy in the most efficient and profitable way. Any government interference with free competition would be counter-productive and harmful to collective.

Social control—controlling what citizens do and what they think. Social control maintains the fabric of our collective. Socialisation or indoctrination is the process by which the collective indoctrinates its members with the formal and informal rules of that collective. Those rules include codes, rites, regulations, doctrines, and laws. They are manmade, and complying with them does not come naturally. The collective establishes and maintains obedience to the rules by reward, punishment, persuasion, ridicule, ostracism, peer pressure, and violence. Socialisation is fostered by social institutions such as schools, corporations, news media, governments, churches, the military, and the justice system. Social control maintains the cohesion of a collective and its culture. See Collective mindmode.

Socrates (470-399 BC)—Greek philosopher, sculptor, and soldier from Athens who was the teacher of Plato and Xenophon. Socrates had a major influence on Western philosophy. By placing emphasis on rational arguments and general definitions, he provided the basis for rational thinking. He also introduced a dialectic style of debate, which holds the pursuit of truth through the interaction of questions and answers. Socrates promoted the objective understanding of concepts such as justice, love, virtue, and self-knowledge. He believed in the superiority of argument over writing and wrote no books himself. In his philosophy, people are inherently good and vice is the result of ignorance. In 399 BC, Socrates was charged by the state and condemned to drink a cup of hemlock. See Greek philosophers.

Solon (630-560 BC)—Greek statesman and businessman who brought the legend of Atlantis from the priest of Sais in Egypt to Greece. See Greek philosophers.

Solution-oriented thinking—focusses on producing correct solutions without sufficiently evaluating the significance of the problems. Solution-oriented thinking finds the right answer for the wrong question. See SCARRED and Conventional thinking.

Space—three-dimensional, infinite, and nonmaterial part of reality in which matter is immersed and moves around. Space provides the exhaustive options to *Advance, Stay, and Retreat*. See Advance, Stay, Retreat, and Sensory reality.

Space-time continuum—Albert Einstein's Theory of Relativity implies that there is no clear-cut distinction between the three dimensions of space and the one dimension of time. Space and time are integrated in a four-dimensional space-time continuum. Although we perceive only three dimensions of space and one of time, physicists have found that some of their mathematical formulae, describing the Universe, require 10 or 26 dimensions in order to remain self-consistent (Kaku, 1994, p. 173). However, the mind perceives naturally three separate dimensions of space and one of time. This perception is the basis for nemonik thinking. See Space, Time, and Nemonik thinking.

Space-time-matter entity—If we accept the hypothesis of physics that inside black-holes, space and time are distorted by the gigantic accumulation of matter, then it is not excluded that matter is an integral part of the space-time continuum. It seems that matter determines the characteristics of space and time. Therefore, there would be no clear distinction between matter and the space-time continuum. In the same way, as there is no clear-cut distinction between space and time. See Space-time continuum.

Spatial—refers to space.

Spatial dimensions—latitude, longitude, and altitude. Together, those coordinates can determine any unique position in space. See Space.

Specialists—peak performers in their field of operation who are exclusively responsible for their personal performance. See Reactive mindmode.

Spencer, Herbert (1820-1903)—English philosopher who introduced the important distinctions between the known, unknown, and unknowable. The creative mindmode deals with the unknown, while the reactive mindmode deals with the known. The unknowable is part of the supernatural reality and is therefore excluded from nemonik thinking. See Nemonik thinking and Supernatural reality.

Spirit—hypothetical nonmaterial part of a person that allegedly provides life to the material body. The spirit is part of the supernatural reality and is therefore excluded from nemonik thinking. See Mind, body and spirit.

Ssu-ma Ch'ien (c. 145-86 BC)—Chinese historian who compiled the *Shih Chi* or Historical Records, which comprised the first comprehensive history of China. Allegedly, Ssu-ma Ch'ien refers to Lao Zi as Li Ehr. See LaoZi and *Dao De Jing*.

Stasis—ultimate state of harmony when the entire Cosmos has become an Oneness or singularity at the end of time. The dynamic *Yin-Yang* balance and all its polarities have disappeared. There will be no dynamism and our reality will not exist anymore. The Way (*Dao*) creates stasis by continuously harmonising the dynamic *Yin-Yang* balance. Nevertheless, stasis might be the onset of a rejuvenation of the dynamic balance. See Harmony, Harmonisation, Restoring the *Yin-Yang* balance, Static balance, LaoZi, and *Dao De Jing*.

Static balance—system in which the opposing polarities are in perfect balance and are not disturbed by external forces. Nevertheless, in our sensory reality the cascade effects of the overall harmonisation will disturb such a static balance. Static balances are therefore temporary. See Stasis, LaoZi, and *Dao De Jing*.

Static thinking—rigid and biased way of thinking that considers only preselected nemoniks and applies those independent of the actual situation. As a result, static thinkers are forced to adjust the situation to their particular way of thinking. Therefore, static thinking is associated with aggression, control, effort, and force. Nevertheless, reality is dynamic and sooner or later, the situation will change. At that moment, any previously productive nemoniks become counterproductive and static thinkers will fail. Antonym—Dynamic thinking. See Conventional thinking and SCARRED.

Stay—spatial nemonik that prompts the mind to maintain the same distance to the goal. Keywords for stay include: broken down, defend, entrench, freeze, halt, idle, immobile, immovable, inactive, inert, inflexible, inoperative, motionless, paralysed, passive, restrain, rigid, space, stable, stagnate, stall, standby, static, stationary, still, stop, unmoving, etc. See Space and Nemoniks.

Strategical thinking—way of thinking that produces strategies. Strategical thinking is incorporated in nemonik thinking. See Prepare and Nemonik thinking.

Strategy—plan to complete a mission, while tactics are detailed plans of that strategy. A complete strategy will comprise decisions about all seventeen nemoniks. Examples of strategies are Blitzkrieg and Scorched Earth. Some consider Napoleon Bonaparte a great strategist. However, Napoleon was biased towards the nemonik to *Advance* and, therefore, lost the Russian campaign and the battle of Waterloo. See Prepare.

Straw dogs (Chinese *chu gou*)—metaphor for non-action. Straw dogs have excellent qualities in Lao Zi's philosophy. If people would act as straw dogs, they would not act at all. In that case, they align with the Way (*Dao*) by following the crucial principle of Non-action. Even sages will apply the principle of Non-action as if they were straw dogs. Hence, Lao Zi's remark about straw dogs is not demeaning in the context of *Dao De Jing.* See Non-action, LaoZi, and *Dao De Jing.*

Strength—intrinsic advantage. For example, having a university degree is strength. Antonym—Weakness. See SWOT analysis.

Strict decision criterion—criterion that will reject information easily. The advantage of a strict decision criterion is that you reject most of the false information. On the other hand, the disadvantage is that you reject too much true information and might become paranoid. Antonym—Lax decision criterion. See Accept.

Subconscious—large part of the mind that is continuously active outside the conscious awareness of that person. The subconscious is associated with sleep, relaxation, knowledge, genius, internal reality, and affectorial thinking. The prime aim of the subconscious is to protect the conscious from an information overload. The resulting mental silence allows the conscious to direct and manage the subconscious. The acquisition of information and creation of mindsets cost much time and effort. Therefore, whether correct or incorrect, subconscious information is precious. Consequently, the subconscious has to protect the acquired information against opposing information. However, this protection of the subconscious could cause close mindedness, cognitive dissonance, extremism, groupthink, and mental stagnation. The subconscious generates affectorial thinking. Antonym—Conscious. See Affectorial thinking, Conscious, Mind, Semiconscious, and Subconscious dominance.

Subconscious dominance—healthy mental state that is fostered by relaxation. During this state, the subconscious is active, while the conscious is inhibited. The aim of this state is mental and physical recuperation. See Conscious dominance, Semiconscious dominance, and Subconscious.

Subjective descriptions—description of reality that depends on the beliefs and perceptions of the particular individual. Alternative descriptions of reality are objective and collective. See Hallucinations, Illusions, Delusions, Mirages, Fata morganas, External reality.

Substance of the universe—Existence is the substance of our Universe. Non-existence is useful, because it maintains this substance. See *Dao*, Existence, LaoZi, and *Dao De Jing*.

Success—*obtain what you seek and escape what you suffer (Lao Zi)*. Some people might seek fame, freedom, knowledge, power, safety, skills, wealth, etc. Others will try to escape ignorance, obscurity, oppression, poverty, violence, weakness, etc. Some might even denounce all desires. Nevertheless, each goal would fit Lao Zi's definition of success. Hence, it is the aim of a healthy mind to maximize success, while survival is the first step of that success. However, incompetent thinkers set the wrong goals and, therefore, they obtain what they suffer most and escape what they need most. The aim of nemonik thinking is maximizing the probability of success. Therefore, nemonik thinking is goal oriented and fosters compassion, allies, and win-win strategies. In contrast, the aim of conventional thinking is maximizing the probability of winning. Antonym—Fail. See Conventional thinking, Nemonik thinking, and Winning.

Successive approximation—cyclic process that moves each turn closer towards the ultimate goal. See Hegel.

Sum-zero-creation—creation in which the sum of all the parts remains zero. In Lao Zi's philosophy, before the formation of the Universe, there was only the Way (*Dao*) in its manifestation of Nothingness. Nothing could be added to it or subtracted from it during the formation, simply because there was nothing else. Therefore, Nothingness remained the same after its division into Existence and Non-existence. Hence, the sum of Existence and Non-existence can only recreate Nothingness. See Supersymmetry, Nothingness, Existence, Non-existence, LaoZi, and *Dao De Jing*.

Sun Tse—See Sun Zi.

Sun Tsu—See Sun Zi.

Sun Wu—See Sun Zi.

Sun Zi (554-496 BC)—Chinese warrior-philosopher who wrote about two-and-half thousand years ago the book— *Bingfa or The Art of War*. Scholars disagree about the personal details of Sun Zi. His real name might have been Sunwu. The name Sun Zi is a phonetic notation of Chinese pictographs and, therefore, his name is alternatively spelled as SunZi, Sunzi, Sun Tsu, SunTzu, Suntzu, Sun Tse, Suntse, Sun Wu, SunWu, Sunwu, etc. See The Art of War and Nemonik thinking.

Suntse—See Sun Zi.

SunTzu—See Sun Zi.

Suntzu—See Sun Zi.

SunWu—See Sun Zi.

Sunwu—See Sun Zi.

SunZi—See Sun Zi.

Sunzi—See Sun Zi.

Super hole—potential merger of all black holes. See Big Crunch.

Superior virtue (Chinese *shang dè*)—synonym for Lao Zi's Natural virtue. See *De*, LaoZi, and *Dao De Jing*.

Supernatural reality—part of the extrasensory reality that is outside the scientific reality. The supernatural reality includes such phenomena as clairvoyance, divine power, ESP, extrasensory perception, God, paranormal, precognition, PSI, psychokinesis, spirit, telekinesis, and telepathy. The supernatural reality is associated with Spencer's concept of the *unknowable*. The supernatural is outside the scope of nemonik thinking. See External reality, Extrasensory reality, Internal reality, Scientific reality, Senses, Sensory reality, and Sensors.

Supernova—nova that alters or destroys the particular star. See Nova.

Supersymmetry—characteristic of the Cosmos in which each participle or force has a mirror participle or force of an equal magnitude and opposing polarity. Lao Zi's theory implies that the Cosmos is a sum-zero-creation and, therefore, it must contain equal amounts of Existence and Non-existence. Existence is the mirror of Non-existence and one cannot exist without the other. See Sum-zero creation, Nothingness, Existence, Non-existence, LaoZi, and *Dao De Jing*.

Survival—process of staying alive, which is the first step of success. See Success.

SWOT-analysis—problem solving tool that evaluates the *Strengths, Weaknesses, Opportunities, and Threats* of each nemonik in comparison to the actual situation. *Strength* is an intrinsic advantage; *Weakness* is an intrinsic disadvantage; *Opportunity* is a potential advantage; and *Threat* is a potential disadvantage. For example, having a university degree is a strength, but receiving a job offer is an opportunity. Having thin bones is a weakness, but the possibility of breaking a leg during skiing is a threat. The SWOT analysis was introduced by the American business consultant Albert S. Humphrey (1926-2005). See Nemonik thinking.

Synergy—additional output that is generated when the interaction between the parts is more than their simple sum. See LaoZi and *Dao De Jing*.

Synthesis—description of reality that merges a thesis and an antithesis into a new thesis. A synthesis might create synergy. See Hegel.

System—organised set of connected material or immaterial entities that form an entirety. A system can be as small as a group of molecules or as large as the entire Universe. See Closed systems and Open systems.

System dependency—over-reliance on organizations, hierarchies, and bureaucracies. See Collective mindmode.

Systems thinking—part of conventional thinking that considers reality to comprise dynamic systems, which influence each other in order to maximize their success. A collective is such a system. See Collective mindmode.

T

Tactic—plan to complete a target in order to maximize success. See Prepare Target.

Tactical thinking—way of thinking that produces tactics in order to maximize success. Tactical thinking is incorporated in nemonik thinking. See Prepare.

Tao (Chinese)—See *Dao*.

Tao Te Ching (Chinese)—See *Dao De Jing*.

Taoism (Chinese)—See *Dao*ism.

TaoTeChing (Chinese)—See *Dao De Jing*.

Taoteching (Chinese)—See *Dao De Jing*.

Target—short-term goal that could be a step towards the completion of a mission. My mission is to make people the best thinkers they can be. Finishing this book is my current target in the completion of my mission. See Prepare and Goal.

Te (Chinese)—See *De*.

Technocrats—people who apply scientific knowledge to develop artefacts such as tools, machines, and computers that increase our control over the environment. See Objective mindmode.

Technology—knowledge and application of artificial manipulation of organic and inorganic matter into artefacts. In our collective, people often regard progress to be the advance of science and the application of more advanced technologies. See Objective mindmode.

Telekinesis—See Supernatural reality.

Telepathy—See Supernatural reality.

Temporal—refers to time.

Thales (c. 624-547 BC)—Greek philosopher who suggested that water was the primordial substance or the origin of all substances. Similarity to Lao Zi's metaphor of water for the Way (Dao). See Greek philosophers, LaoZi, and Dao De Jing.

The Art of War or Bing Fa—book about strategy written by Sun Zi about two-and-half thousand years ago. Although written about war, Sun Zi's advice applies also to daily life. Bing Fa is a phonetic notation of Chinese pictographs and, therefore, it is alternatively spelled as Bingfa, Pingfa, Ping Fa, etc. See Abstract of the Art of War.

The Way—See Dao (Chinese).

The Way of Nature—See Dao (Chinese).

The Way of People—See De (Chinese).

Theory of the Cosmos—Lao Zi's cosmological theory holds that during the first division, the nameless void of desolate empty Nothingness (Dao) was simultaneously divided into Existence and Non-existence. Existence and Non-existence are equal but opposing polarities and, therefore their sum can only recreate Nothingness or zero. This sum-zero-creation might underlie a supersymmetry in which each participle or force has a mirror participle or force of an equal magnitude and opposing polarity. See Sum-zero creation, Supersymmetry, Nothingness, Existence, Non-existence, LaoZi, and Dao De Jing.

Thermodynamics—See First Law of Thermodynamics.

Thesis—tested description of reality. See Hegel.

Thinking—self-organizing mental process that recalls, evaluates, transforms, and generates information. The quality of your thinking determines your education, mental and physical wellbeing, socio-economic status, and the overall quality and duration of your life. It determines whether you are at war or live in peace. Your thinking determines everything worth living for. See Conventional thinking and Nemonik thinking.

Third division—division of the Three into All-things. In Lao Zi's philosophy, the Three are: The Sky, the Earth and the King or the people. Together they create All-things, which are the myriad of organic and inorganic things that exist in the sensory reality. See First division, Second division, Oneness, Two, Three, All-things, *Dao*, Nothingness, Existence, Non-existence, LaoZi, and *Dao De Jing*.

Third Law of Motion—every action evokes a reaction of equal magnitude and opposite direction. In Lao Zi's philosophy, any disturbance of a *Yin-Yang* balance will be restored by the Way (*Dao*) in its manifestation as *Qi*. Hence, the Third Law of Motion formalizes Lao Zi's ideas. See Newton, First law, Second law, LaoZi, and *Dao De Jing*.

Threat—potential disadvantage. A threat is optional and the outcome depends on the decision of the person. For example, breaking a leg during skiing is a threat. Antonym—Opportunity. See SWOT-analysis.

Three (Chinese *san*)—refers to the three Greatnesses of the second division of the formation of the Universe: The Sky, the Earth and the King or the people (Lao Zi). See First division, Second division, Third division, Oneness, Two, All-things, *Dao*, Nothingness, Existence, Non-existence, LaoZi, and *Dao De Jing*.

Three fundamental alignments—Maintaining the *Yin-Yang* balance; Aligning with Harmonisations; and Restoring the *Yin-Yang* balance (Lao Zi). These fundamental alignments were derived from the possible options of sages to align with the Way (*Dao*). See Maintaining the *Yin-Yang* balance, Aligning with harmonisations, Restoring the *Yin-Yang* balance, LaoZi, and *Dao De Jing.*

Three stages of the formation—Oneness is the manifestation of the Way (*Dao*) as the Nameless void of desolate empty Nothingness, which is the origin of the Universe (Lao Zi). We may reduce Lao Zi's four stages of the formation of the Universe to three: *"The One generated the Two; the Two generated the Three; and the Three generated All-things."* See LaoZi and *Dao De Jing.*

Three treasures (Chinese *san bao*)—frugality, humility and compassion (Lao Zi). Maintaining the *Yin-Yang* balance includes frugality; Aligning with the harmonisations includes humility and Restoring the *Yin-Yang* balance includes compassion. See LaoZi and *Dao De Jing.*

Tian (Chinese)—See Sky.

Timaeus—See Plato.

Time—one-dimensional, eternal, and nonmaterial part of reality that can be perceived indirectly by changes in matter and the movement of matter through space. Time provides the exhaustive nemoniks to *Act, Wait, and Prepare.* See Space, Matter, and Sensory reality.

Timing—execution of an action at the most productive moment. See Act and Wait.

Traditional thinking—See Conventional thinking.

Tranquillity (Chinese *jing*)—See Harmony.

Transformation—simultaneous accumulation of one type of matter by disposing another type of matter. See Matter.

Treasures—See Three treasures.

True—description of reality that is consistent with the sensory reality. See True arguments.

True arguments—consistent, reliable, and valid logical arguments. See Logical argument.

Truisms—See Aphorisms.

Two (Chinese *liang*)—refers to Existence and Non-existence (Lao Zi). Those were generated during the first division of the formation of the Universe. Incorrectly, some have explained that the Two refers to *Yin* and *Yang*. However, *Yin* and *Yang* are associated with All-things, which is the lowest entity in the hierarchy of the formation of the Universe. See First division, Second division, Third division, Oneness, Three, All-things, *Dao*, Nothingness, Existence, Non-existence, LaoZi, and *Dao De Jing*.

U

Uncarved block—See Simplicity.

Unconsciousness—unhealthy mental state that is characterized by a persistent unawareness of the sensory reality and the Self. Unconsciousness differs from subconscious dominance, because you will not wake up in case of danger. Hence, unconsciousness could be seen as a suspension of life. Unconsciousness could be caused by physical or mental traumas, analgesics, asphyxiation, and toxic substances. See Conscious, Mind, Semiconscious, and Subconscious.

Unified field theory for physics—account simultaneously for the gravitational, electromagnetic, and weak and strong nuclear forces. Although physicists might be close to the completion of this theory, the Universe is full of surprises. The recent discovery that the expansion of the Universe is still accelerating supports the existence of 'dark energy' (Leitl; 3-12-1999). Including this new energy in the unified field theory might increase the problem considerably. See Objective mindmode.

Universal Law of Causality—natural law that prevails in daily life and holds that the same natural cause always precedes the same natural effect. This law assumes order in the Universe. See Objective mindmode.

Universe (Chinese *guo*)—that part of Nothingness, which forms the sensory reality comprising matter, energy, space and time. The Universe of our reality is created by the division of Nothingness into Existence and Non-existence (Lao Zi). It is not excluded that there is also a parallel or anti-Universe that comprises negative celestial bodies, energy, space, and time. *'Universe'* seems to be a more appropriate interpretation of the Chinese *guo* than *'country'*. See Anti-universe, LaoZi, and *Dao De Jing*.

Unknowable—See Spencer.

Unknown—See Spencer.

Unrealistic thinking—way of thinking that is inconsistent with the sensory reality. Unrealistic thinking differs from non-rational thinking. See Sensory reality and Nemonik thinking.

V

Valid arguments—comprise facts that are related to the conclusion that they intend to support. In the argument (A > B, B > C, therefore ...), (A > X would be an invalid conclusion, because X is not mentioned in the facts). See Logical arguments.

Validity—measure of how well a theory applies to the topic of that theory. Validity refers to measuring the correct variable. See Reliability.

Valley (Chinese *yu*)—metaphor for the Way.

Vertical thinking—way of rational thinking that solves problems by overcoming obstacles in the chosen line of approach. This concept was introduced by Edward de Bono as the opposite of lateral thinking. Antonym—Lateral thinking. See Edward de Bono, Conventional thinking, and Rational thinking.

Vibrating phenomenon—some physicists suggest that the Big Bang was the physical start of the formation of our Universe. That huge explosion explains the expansion of our Universe and why galaxies are moving apart. If there is insufficient matter in the Universe then there is not enough gravity to contract all that matter back into one point. In that case, the Universe is open and its expansion will go on forever. If there is sufficient matter in the Universe, then it is closed and sooner or later, the expansion will decelerate into a contraction or Big Crunch. The Cosmos might be a dynamic and continuous process of expansion and contraction. See Nothingness, LaoZi, and *Dao De Jing*.

Vinci—See da Vinci.

Virtue—See *De* (Chinese).

Virus—small entity that lives in a host and is concealed, self-replicating, and self-protective. A benign virus lives in symbiosis within its host, while a malignant virus destroys its host.

Visual spatial perception—conscious three-dimensional perception of space that is created subconsciously by integrating the different pictures that are perceived by each eye. See Perception.

Visualization—mental picture that is consciously maintained in the internal reality in order to inhibit unintentional conscious thoughts during mediation. See Nemonik meditation.

Vital energy—See *Qi*.

Void—See Nothingness.

W

Wait—temporal nemonik that prompts the mind to delay an action until it is the right time for that action. Keywords for wait include: adjourn, break, breather, defer, delay, patience, pause, postpone, procrastinate, put on hold, recess, respite, rest, stand, stall, suspend, time, time off, timeout, timing, etc. See Nemoniks and Time.

Wan wu (Chinese)—See All-things.

Wang (Chinese)—See King.

Warring States (475-221 BC)—period of continuous warfare in China. This influential and fertile period was preceded by the Spring and Autumn period (770-476 BC) when China comprised many small states. In 223 BC, the state Chin finally defeated Chu and the period of Warring States ended with the unification of Chin and Chu in 221 BC.

Water (shui)—metaphor for the Way (*Dao*).

Way—See *Dao* (Chinese)

Way of least resistance—achieving success in the most efficient way. In Lao Zi's philosophy, if we have to use effort or encounter resistance, we are opposing the Way (*Dao*) and we will perish. Sages foster efficiency, Non-action, and Affectorial thinking. Drift with the flow of the water, go with the wind, and the unstoppable force of the Way will be with you. See Effort, LaoZi, and *Dao De Jing*.

Way of Nature—See *Dao*.

Way of the People—See *De*.

Way of the Sages—See *De*.

Weakness—intrinsic disadvantage. For example, having thin bones is a weakness. Antonym—Strength. See SWOT-analysis.

Winning—defeating opponents in competition and, therefore, winning is conflict oriented, which fosters control, force, aggression, enemies, and win-lose strategies. The aim of conventional thinking is maximizing the probability of winning. In contrast, the aim of nemonik thinking is maximizing the probability of success. Antonym—Losing. See Conventional thinking.

Wisdom—productive application of knowledge to the actual situation. Wisdom is our mental resonance with nature. See SCARRED and Nemonik thinking.

Wooden block—See Simplicity.

Wu (Chinese)—See Non-existence.

Wu Ji (Chinese)—See Moderation.

Wu ming (Chinese)—See Nameless.

Wu ming pu (Chinese)—See Nameless Simplicity.

Wu wei (Chinese)—See Non-action.

X

Xenophon (430-354 BC)—Greek historian, philosopher, and soldier Student of Socrates. Although associated with Sparta, he was also known as Xenophon of Athens.

Xia de (Chinese)—Inferior virtue.

Xiao (Chinese)—See Desolate.

Xu xin (Chinese)—See Empty mind.

Xuan pin (Chinese)—See Mysterious Female.

Y

Yang (Chinese)—literally the sunny side of the hill. However, in the context of Chinese bipolar philosophy, *Yang* means also the rational mind, male, front, positive, firm, above, open, overt, dry, active, etc. In Lao Zi's philosophy, *Yang* is the manifestation of Existence in our reality and the complementary opposite of *Yin*. Antonym—*Yin*. See Archetype of *Yang*, Existence, Non-existence, *Yin*, *Dao*, *Qi*, LaoZi, and *Dao De Jing*.

Yang thinking—See Rational thinking.

Yi (Chinese)—See Justice.

Yi (Chinese)—See Oneness.

Yin (Chinese)—literally the shady side of the hill. However, in the context of Chinese bipolar philosophy, *Yin* means also the intuitive mind, the female, the back, negative, yielding, below, hidden, secret, moist, passive, etc. In Lao Zi's philosophy, *Yin* is the manifestation of Non-existence in our reality and the complementary opposite of *Yang*. Antonym—*Yang*. See Archetype of *Yin*, Existence, Non-existence, *Yin*, *Dao*, *Qi*, LaoZi, and *Dao De Jing*.

Yin thinking—See Affectorial thinking.

Yin-Yang balance—dynamic balance manifesting the cosmological balance between Non-existence and Existence in the sensory reality. As the sum of Existence and Non-existence equals zero or Nothingness, the Way has to maintain both balances because Nothingness cannot increase or decrease. See Dynamic balance, LaoZi, and *Dao De Jing*.

You ming (Chinese)—See Naming.

Young, Thomas (1773-1829)—conducted the famous double-split experiment that supported the widely accepted antithesis that light moves through space like a wave. This antithesis contradicted Newton's thesis that light comprised small particles. Einstein synthesized those ideas. See Einstein, Newton, Young, Hegel, and Scientists.

Yu (Chinese)—See Valley.

Yu shen bu si (Chinese)—See Immortal Valley Spirit.

Z

Zen Buddhism—school of Buddhism that developed in China and spread later to Japan. The aim of Zen is to see the world as it is. Live in the now and here. The ultimate state of nirvana can be reached in a single lifetime, rather than in a succession of value accumulating lives. Zen doctrine holds that the distinction between things is just an illusion, which is the same as Lao Tzu's concept of the manifestation of the Way (*Dao*) as the undivided Oneness or Nameless. Zen Buddhism adopted Lao Tzu's method of teaching without many words. Zen in the highest form is wordless. To reach that level of awareness, the Zen master will ask the novice to solve a set of koans that inhibit rational thinking. See Koan, Affectorial thinking, Lao Zi, and *Dao De Jing*.

Zhi (Chinese)—See Knowledge.

Zhi de (Chinese)—See Natural virtue.

Zone—See Silent mind.

APPENDICES

Notes

_____

_____

_____

_____

_____

_____

_____

_____

_____

_____

_____

_____

BIBLIOGRAPHY

Schade, A. (2015). bioPAD: Nemonik Thinking (PowerPoint). Dunedin: nemonik-thinking.org.

Schade, A. (2016). *Dictionary for Nemonik Thinking.* nemonik-thinking.org.

Schade, A. (2016). *Global Warming is the Solution.* nemonik-thinking.org.

Schade, A. (2016). *Think Smarter with Nemonik Thinking.* nemonik-thinking.org.

Schade, A. (planned 2017). *Lao Zi's True Dao De Jing.* nemonik-thinking.org.

Schade, A. (planned 2017). *Sun Zi's The Art of War.* nemonik-thinking.org.

Schade, A. (planned 2017). *The Unreal Reality.* nemonik-thinking.org.

Notes

ABSTRACTS OTHER BOOKS

THINK SMARTER...

Think Smarter with Nemonik Thinking (Schade, 2016). This is the operating manual for your mind that you should have received at birth. Nemonik thinking is a smarter way of thinking that aims to maximize your success by evaluating seventeen nemoniks, which are memorized keywords describing all the perceived aspects of your mind, reality, and their interaction. Success is obtaining what you seek and escaping what you suffer. Therefore, it is goal oriented. To maximize your success, nemonik thinking mobilizes your hidden genius, accelerates your thinking, improves your memory, reveals opportunities and threats, creates questions and ideas, and reduces your stress levels. It is like playing a musical keyboard with seventeen keys producing an infinite repertoire of smart strategies. Nemonik thinking is unique because it is the first exhaustive and transferable way of thinking. Comparisons with Sir Richard Branson's way of thinking show that it is extremely productive. Unfortunately, the educational system conditions students still with pass-fail grades to win. Winning is defeating opponents in competition. Therefore, it is conflict oriented. The compulsion to win inhibits the truth and, therefore, fosters the corrupted way of conventional thinking. Conventional thinking creates the malignant cognitive virus CS7. In turn, that virus consolidates conventional thinking with cognitive dissonance and groupthink. Conventional thinking is time consuming. Hence, the less time you have, the greater the necessity to study nemonik thinking. You might be the best thinker in the world, but only nemonik thinking could make you the smartest thinker you can be.

Download a free eBook version
@ nemonik-thinking.org

DICTIONARY...

Dictionary Nemonik Thinking (Schade 2016). Nemonik thinking mobilizes your hidden genius, accelerates your thinking,
improves your memory, reveals opportunities and threats,
creates questions and ideas, and reduces your stress levels.
Nemonik thinking divides the mind into 17 nemonik regions.
Those regions defragment information, which facilitates the
storage, maintenance, recall, and processing of associated information from memory. However, the boundaries of those
nemonik regions are fuzzy. Therefore, the aim of this dictionary is to differentiate them by providing keywords for
each nemonik concept. The first part of this dictionary trans-
lates nemonik concepts into common keywords (e.g. *advance*
into attack, bypass, etc.). In contrast, the second part trans-
lates common keywords into nemonik concepts (e.g. attack,
bypass, etc. into *advance*). This dictionary shows that the
complexity of conventional thinking comprises thousands of
keywords that can be simplified to 17 nemoniks. This reduction will increase the speed of your thinking. To become
skilled in nemonik thinking, it is recommended to study—
Think Smarter with Nemonik Thinking (Schade, 2016).

GLOBAL WARMING...

Global Warming is the Solution (Schade 2016). This study presents a bilateral synthesis of artificial global warming and natural global cooling. Mainstream climatology lacks scientific integrity and statistical methodology. Peer review is changed into peer pressure and objectors are labelled *"Deniers"*. Proper statistical analyses are replaced by graphs and non-causal correlation analyses that are based on the last 166 years, while 420,000 years of Antarctic data are mainly discarded. Furthermore, climatology ignores that 400 ppm of CO_2 predicts a global temperature of 11.5 °C, rather than the current 1.3 °C. It focuses on artificial global warming and overlooks the threat of natural global cooling. It also ignores the solar expert Professor Zharkova, who predicts a mini ice-age by 2030, which is likely to turn global warming into global cooling. The current study compared the Antarctic temperatures during the last 10,000 years (baseline 0.00 °C) with the global temperature of 1.3 °C. This common definition of global warming failed to reach statistical significance. However, the Antarctic temperatures during the last 420.000 years support the notion that we live in a glacial period of -8.9 °C, rather than in an interglacial period of 0.00 °C. In that case, the artificial global warming would be 10.2 °C, rather than 1.3 °C. This alternative definition of global warming is statistically significant. Furthermore, it is supported by the current CO_2 level of 400 ppm and the significant duration and stability of the current interglacial. Consequently, decreasing the CO_2 level could cause a global disaster threatening the survival of humanity. The increased thermal range and the precarious balance between artificial global warming and natural global cooling could also explain the current climatological instability.

LAO ZI'S DAO DE JING

Lao Zi's Dao De Jing—The Way (Schade, planned 2017). In one curt sentence, Lao Zi explains the core of his book—Use it to obtain what you seek and to escape what you suffer. His inspirational guideline introduces the sophisticated yet simple principle of *Dao.* This principle explains the Universe, the meaning of life, and our place in nature. For more than two and a half thousand years, *Dao De Jing* has been shrouded in mystery. Many scholars have studied that intriguing manuscript by peeling away layer after layer of meaning to unravel its cryptic secrets. Nevertheless, this interpretation shows that *Dao De Jing* preserved its ancient secrets within a prosaic collection of aphorisms. These mysteries are revealed for the first time ever in a clearly understandable way, imparting forgotten knowledge about the Universe and the art of living. To become skilled in nemonik thinking, it is recommended to study—*Think Smarter with Nemonik Thinking (Schade, 2016).*

SUN ZI'S THE ART OF WAR

Sun Zi's Bin Fa—The Art of War (Schade, planned 2017). Sun Zi (554-496 BC) was a Chinese warrior-philosopher who wrote the military classic *Bing Fa* or *The Art of War.* Although his book is about war, his strategies apply to every facet of daily life. Sun Zi deals with the art of positioning yourself in space, matter, and time. He addresses the questions raised by nemonik thinking of where, what, and when to advance, stay, retreat, accumulate, preserve, dispose, act, wait, prepare, accept, reject, reveal, and conceal. Think smarter and incorporate Sun Zi's strategies in your thinking. To become skilled in nemonik thinking, it is recommended to study—*Think Smarter with Nemonik Thinking (Schade, 2016).*

Notes

_____

_____

_____

_____

_____

_____

_____

_____

_____

_____

_____

_____

COVER DESIGN

The mirror images on the front and back of the cover illustrate the intentional emptiness of this manual. This manual is referred to as *empty* because nemonik thinking is not fostering or inhibiting any cult, doctrine, dogma, ideology, or religion. Nemonik thinking generates questions and ideas, rather than answers or opinions. Responses to those questions and ideas depend on the actual situation and the belief system of the thinker. Nemonik thinking is a neutral mental skill that activates your thinking. It is about how to think, rather than what to believe. Seeing a deeper meaning in it is a clear misunderstanding concerning the essence of nemonik thinking.

DECLARATION OF INDEPENDENCE

I, Dr Auke Schade, declare that this study and the development of nemonik thinking were funded by private resources. No part of this study, or the development of nemonik thinking, was supported, financially or otherwise, by any third party including individuals, stakeholders, charities, commercial, academic, political, ideological, military, religious, and secret organizations. Consequently, I am an independent researcher and do not have to please anyone.

The main global problems are symptoms of humanity's dramatically failing way of thinking. Although a huge and immediate threat, climate change is only one of the many symptoms. Seen the lethargic response of leaders to global warming, it would be unwise to rely on the global establishment for adequate action. Turning the tide in time will require huge sacrifices and resources. Therefore, support from any individual or organisation will be welcomed, as long as it will not comprise my academic integrity.

Now, after the completion of this study and the development of nemonik thinking, I feel even free to approach the oil and coal industries for funding. Confirmation of the bilateral climate-change hypothesis would transform them from villains into heroes. Their industrial CO_2 might save us from living on a frozen planet.

Donations Welcome!

WEBSITE

It is the aim of the website *nemonik-thinking.org* to provide interactive on-line information about nemonik thinking. This includes discussions, books, blog, videos, exercises, updates, activities, web links, and tests. Join the nemonik thinkers and receive the latest updates. It is a work in progress. Check it out and have your say! I look forward to your feedback at:

nemonik-thinking.org